THE CAMBRIDGE ELEMENTARY MATHEMATICAL

COMPILED AND ARRANGED FOR THE
CAMBRIDGE LOCAL EXAMINATIONS SYNDICATE
BY J. C. P. MILLER AND F. C. POWELL
Second edition

CONTENTS

CAMBRIDGE UNIVERSITY PRESS

CAMBRIDGE

LONDON NEW YORK NEW ROCHELLE

MELBOURNE SYDNEY

NOTES ON THE USE OF THE TABLES

The tabulated values. A mathematical table gives the values of a function for a number of values of the independent variable x. Usually these values are evenly spaced, but in some tables the tabulation interval varies. Thus in the table of reciprocals the tabulation interval is 0.001 for $x < 1.5$, 0.01 for $1.5 < x < 6$ and 0.1 for $x > 6$.

In many tables the tabular values are arranged in rows. To illustrate the use of such a table we consider the evaluation of 3.47^2. Turning to the table of squares we first find the appropriate row by looking for the leading digits (34) in the x-column, and then move across to the column headed by the next digit (7). The required value is seen to be 12.04. In other tables the tabular values are arranged in columns.

Tabular values are usually rounded, not exact, and so may be in error by $\frac{1}{2}$ unit in the last figure. Thus the true value of 3.47^2 lies between 12.035 and 12.045; it is not exactly 12.04.

Interpolation. This is a process for finding the values of a function for intermediate values of the independent variable. The simplest, *linear interpolation*, is based on the assumption that the function changes at a constant rate between one tabular value y_1 and the next, y_2. Denote the corresponding values of x by x_1 and x_2, and put $x_2 = x_1 + h$, $y_2 = y_1 + \Delta$; here h is *the tabular interval* and Δ is *the difference* between successive tabular values of the function. For the intermediate value $x_1 + ph$ ($0 < p < 1$), the value of the function is taken to be $y_1 + p\Delta$. The increment $p\Delta$ is called *the proportional part* (PP) of the difference Δ. Differences and their PPs are usually rounded to whole numbers of units in the last figure or decimal place.

For an increasing function PPs must be added, but for a decreasing function they must be subtracted.

Consider for instance the evaluation of 3.088^2. From the table of squares (an increasing function) $3.08^2 = 9.486$ and $3.09^2 = 9.548$, so $\Delta = 62$ units. The required PP is 0.8×62 or 50 units to the nearest whole number. The approximate value of 3.088^2 is thus $9.486 + 50$ units or 9.536. (The true value is 9.535744.)

In some tables, where the tabular values are arranged in columns, differences are shown in small print to the right of the tabular values.

Since the rounding of a PP may introduce a further error of $\frac{1}{2}$ unit, the total error in this mode of interpolation may amount to 1 unit. (A further error may arise from non-linearity, as explained below.)

For convenience a table of proportional parts, rounded to whole numbers, for the fractions $p = 0.1, 0.2, \ldots, 0.9$ is given on p. 45.

Mean proportional parts. Often Δ does not vary much along a row. A single set of PPs is then provided, and can be used without serious error instead of the PPs of the true differences. These mean PPs are placed to the right of each row of function values.

The use of mean PPs may give rise to an additional error of 1 unit, making a total error of 2 units. This is sufficiently accurate for many practical purposes.

By using the given mean PPs we obtain for 3.088^2 the value $9.486 + 49$ units or 9.535. This differs by 1 unit from the value found above.

Where the differences in a row would vary too widely the row may be broken into two or more parts, each part-row being then given its own set of mean PPs.

Where no mean PPs are given, linear interpolation based on PPs of true differences may be used except where interpolation is stated to be unreliable.

Non-linearity. The assumption that the value of the function changes at a constant rate leads to errors that become serious if Δ changes rapidly. The error due to non-linearity is greatest where $p = \frac{1}{2}$ and is then $\frac{1}{8}S$, where S (*the second difference*) is the difference between two successive values of Δ. Where PPs are provided for an unbroken row this error is negligible. Where PPs are provided for a broken row it cannot exceed $\frac{1}{4}$ unit.

This contribution to error must be kept in mind when interpolating by use of PPs of the true difference, especially where mean PPs cannot be provided owing to the rapid variation of Δ, or, for functions tabulated in columns, where Δ is not given. If, for example, $S = 12$ the total error (made up from tabulation errors, error in rounding the PP, and error due to non-linearity) may amount to $2\frac{1}{2}$ units. Linear interpolation becomes unreliable if S exceeds 12, and it may be necessary to drop the last figure (which reduces differences by a factor 10) or to use another method.

Double use of proportional parts. Consider the evaluation of lg 1.6716. From the table lg 1.67 = 0.2227, lg 1.68 = 0.2253, and so the difference Δ corresponding to the tabular interval $h = 0.01$ is 26 units. The correct PP is therefore 0.16 × 26 or, to the nearest whole number, 4 units, giving for lg 1.6716 the value 0.2227 + 4 units or 0.2231. (The true value is approximately 0.22313.)

A more convenient but less accurate method is as follows:

lg 1.67	= 0.2227
PP for 0.1 h =	3 units
PP for 0.06 h =	1.6 units, i.e. $\frac{1}{10}$ (PP for 0.6 h)
lg 1.6716	= 0.22316 or 0.2232 to 4 decimal places

Since this method involves rounding *two* PPs it is liable to an additional error of $\frac{1}{2}$ unit.

Summary of interpolation errors

Method	$S = 0$	2	4	8	12
Tabular values	$\frac{1}{2}$	$\frac{1}{2}$	$\frac{1}{2}$	$\frac{1}{2}$	$\frac{1}{2}$
PPs of true differences	1	$1\frac{1}{4}$	$1\frac{1}{2}$	2	$2\frac{1}{2}$
Mean PPs for unbroken rows	2	—	—	—	—
Mean PPs for broken rows	—	$2\frac{1}{4}$	—	—	—
Double use of PPs	add $\frac{1}{2}$				

Simultaneous use of two functions

Examples (i) *To find* $\sqrt{(1 - u^2)}$ when $u = 0.54$. If $u = \sin x$, we need cos x. From the table on p. 35:

(for $x = 0.57$)   sin $x = 0.5396$, $\Delta_S = 84$ cos $x = 0.8419$, $\Delta_C = -54$

so

$$\sqrt{(1 - u^2)} = \cos \sin^{-1}u = 0.8419 - (4/84) \times 54 \times 0.0001$$
$$= 0.8419 - 0.00026 \simeq 0.8416$$

(ii) *To find* $u^{3/2}$ when $u = 7630$. If $u = x^2$ we need x^3. Now from the table on p. 29:

(for $x = 87$) $x^2 = 7569$, $\Delta_2 = 175$ $x^3 = 6585 \times 10^2$, $\Delta_3 = 230$

(We retain only 4 figures in x^3 in order to reduce second differences.) Since $7630 - 7569 = 61$, the required value is:

$$\{6585 + (61/175) \times 230\} \times 10^2 \approx 6.665 \times 10^5$$

Other functions that can be evaluated in a similar way include $u^{1/6}$ ($= (u^{1/2})^{1/3}$), $u^{2/3}$ ($= (u^2)^{1/3}$), $u^{1/4}$, $\sqrt{(1 + u^2)}$ ($= \cosh (\sinh^{-1}u)$ or sec $(\tan^{-1}u)$), $\sqrt{(u^2 - 1)}$, $u/\sqrt{(1 + u^2)}$ ($= \tanh (\sinh^{-1}u)$ or sin $(\tan^{-1}u)$).

LOGARITHMS, BASE 10 $\log_{10}x$ or lg x

x	0	1	2	3	4	5	6	7	8	9	1	2	3	4	5	6	7	8	9
														ADD					
10	.0000	0043	0086	0128	0170	0212	0253	0294	0334	0374	4	8	13	17	21	25	29	34	38
											4	8	12	16	20	24	28	32	36
11	.0414	0453	0492	0531	0569	0607	0645	0682	0719	0755	4	8	12	16	19	23	27	31	35
											4	7	11	15	19	22	26	30	33
12	.0792	0828	0864	0899	0934	0969	1004	1038	1072	1106	4	7	11	14	18	21	25	28	32
											3	7	10	14	17	20	24	27	31
13	.1139	1173	1206	1239	1271	1303	1335	1367	1399	1430	3	7	10	13	16	20	23	26	30
											3	6	10	13	16	19	22	26	29
14	.1461	1492	1523	1553	1584	1614	1644	1673	1703	1732	3	6	9	12	15	18	21	24	27
15	.1761	1790	1818	1847	1875	1903	1931	1959	1987	2014	3	6	8	11	14	17	20	22	25
16	.2041	2068	2095	2122	2148	2175	2201	2227	2253	2279	3	5	8	10	13	16	18	21	23
17	.2304	2330	2355	2380	2405	2430	2455	2480	2504	2529	2	5	7	10	12	15	17	20	22
18	.2553	2577	2601	2625	2648	2672	2695	2718	2742	2765	2	5	7	10	12	14	17	19	22
19	.2788	2810	2833	2856	2878	2900	2923	2945	2967	2989	2	4	6	9	11	13	15	18	20
20	.3010	3032	3054	3075	3096	3118	3139	3160	3181	3201	2	4	6	8	11	13	15	17	19
21	.3222	3243	3263	3284	3304	3324	3345	3365	3385	3404	2	4	6	8	10	12	14	16	18
22	.3424	3444	3464	3483	3502	3522	3541	3560	3579	3598	2	4	6	8	10	11	13	15	17
23	.3617	3636	3655	3674	3692	3711	3729	3747	3766	3784	2	4	5	7	9	11	13	14	16
24	.3802	3820	3838	3856	3874	3892	3909	3927	3945	3962	2	4	5	7	9	11	13	14	16
25	.3979	3997	4014	4031	4048	4065	4082	4099	4116	4133	2	3	5	7	9	10	12	14	15
26	.4150	4166	4183	4200	4216	4232	4249	4265	4281	4298	2	3	5	6	8	10	11	13	14
27	.4314	4330	4346	4362	4378	4393	4409	4425	4440	4456	2	3	5	6	8	10	11	13	14
28	.4472	4487	4502	4518	4533	4548	4564	4579	4594	4609	2	3	5	6	8	9	11	12	14
29	.4624	4639	4654	4669	4683	4698	4713	4728	4742	4757	1	3	4	6	7	9	10	12	13
30	.4771	4786	4800	4814	4829	4843	4857	4871	4886	4900	1	3	4	6	7	8	10	11	13
31	.4914	4928	4942	4955	4969	4983	4997	5011	5024	5038	1	3	4	6	7	8	10	11	13
32	.5051	5065	5079	5092	5105	5119	5132	5145	5159	5172	1	3	4	5	7	8	9	10	12
33	.5185	5198	5211	5224	5237	5250	5263	5276	5289	5302	1	3	4	5	6	8	9	10	12
34	.5315	5328	5340	5353	5366	5378	5391	5403	5416	5428	1	3	4	5	6	8	9	10	12
35	.5441	5453	5465	5478	5490	5502	5514	5527	5539	5551	1	2	4	5	6	7	8	10	11
36	.5563	5575	5587	5599	5611	5623	5635	5647	5658	5670	1	2	4	5	6	7	8	10	11
37	.5682	5694	5705	5717	5729	5740	5752	5763	5775	5786	1	2	4	5	6	7	8	10	11
38	.5798	5809	5821	5832	5843	5855	5866	5877	5888	5899	1	2	3	4	6	7	8	9	10
39	.5911	5922	5933	5944	5955	5966	5977	5988	5999	6010	1	2	3	4	6	7	8	9	10
40	.6021	6031	6042	6053	6064	6075	6085	6096	6107	6117	1	2	3	4	5	7	8	9	10
41	.6128	6138	6149	6160	6170	6180	6191	6201	6212	6222	1	2	3	4	5	6	7	8	9
42	.6232	6243	6253	6263	6274	6284	6294	6304	6314	6325	1	2	3	4	5	6	7	8	9
43	.6335	6345	6355	6365	6375	6385	6395	6405	6415	6425	1	2	3	4	5	6	7	8	9
44	.6435	6444	6454	6464	6474	6484	6493	6503	6513	6522	1	2	3	4	5	6	7	8	9
45	.6532	6542	6551	6561	6571	6580	6590	6599	6609	6618	1	2	3	4	5	6	7	8	9
46	.6628	6637	6646	6656	6665	6675	6684	6693	6702	6712	1	2	3	4	5	5	6	7	8
47	.6721	6730	6739	6749	6758	6767	6776	6785	6794	6803	1	2	3	4	5	5	6	7	8
48	.6812	6821	6830	6839	6848	6857	6866	6875	6884	6893	1	2	3	4	4	5	6	7	8
49	.6902	6911	6920	6928	6937	6946	6955	6964	6972	6981	1	2	3	4	4	5	6	7	8

Examples:

lg $3.674 = 0.5647 + 0.0005 = 0.5652$
lg $367.4 = \lg(3.674 \times 10^2) = 2.5652$
lg $0.003674 = \lg(3.674 \times 10^{-3}) = \bar{3}.5652$

Constant	π	e	lg e	ln 10
Value	3.14159	2.71828	0.43429	2.30259
log (base 10)	0.49715	0.43429	$\bar{1}.63778$	0.36222

LOGARITHMS, BASE 10 $\log_{10}x$ or $\lg x$

x	0	1	2	3	4	5	6	7	8	9	1	2	3	4	5	6	7	8	9
															ADD				
50	.6990	6998	7007	7016	7024	7033	7042	7050	7059	7067	1	2	3	4	4	5	6	7	8
51	.7076	7084	7093	7101	7110	7118	7126	7135	7143	7152	1	2	2	3	4	5	6	6	7
52	.7160	7168	7177	7185	7193	7202	7210	7218	7226	7235	1	2	2	3	4	5	6	6	7
53	.7243	7251	7259	7267	7275	7284	7292	7300	7308	7316	1	2	2	3	4	5	6	6	7
54	.7324	7332	7340	7348	7356	7364	7372	7380	7388	7396	1	2	2	3	4	5	6	6	7
55	.7404	7412	7419	7427	7435	7443	7451	7459	7466	7474	1	2	2	3	4	5	6	6	7
56	.7482	7490	7497	7505	7513	7520	7528	7536	7543	7551	1	2	2	3	4	5	6	6	7
57	.7559	7566	7574	7582	7589	7597	7604	7612	7619	7627	1	2	2	3	4	5	6	6	7
58	.7634	7642	7649	7657	7664	7672	7679	7686	7694	7701	1	2	2	3	4	5	6	6	7
59	.7709	7716	7723	7731	7738	7745	7752	7760	7767	7774	1	1	2	3	4	4	5	6	6
60	.7782	7789	7796	7803	7810	7818	7825	7832	7839	7846	1	1	2	3	4	4	5	6	6
61	.7853	7860	7868	7875	7882	7889	7896	7903	7910	7917	1	1	2	3	4	4	5	6	6
62	.7924	7931	7938	7945	7952	7959	7966	7973	7980	7987	1	1	2	3	3	4	5	6	6
63	.7993	8000	8007	8014	8021	8028	8035	8041	8048	8055	1	1	2	3	3	4	5	6	6
64	.8062	8069	8075	8082	8089	8096	8102	8109	8116	8122	1	1	2	3	3	4	5	6	6
65	.8129	8136	8142	8149	8156	8162	8169	8176	8182	8189	1	1	2	3	3	4	5	6	6
66	.8195	8202	8209	8215	8222	8228	8235	8241	8248	8254	1	1	2	3	3	4	5	6	6
67	.8261	8267	8274	8280	8287	8293	8299	8306	8312	8319	1	1	2	2	3	4	4	5	5
68	.8325	8331	8338	8344	8351	8357	8363	8370	8376	8382	1	1	2	2	3	4	4	5	5
69	.8388	8395	8401	8407	8414	8420	8426	8432	8439	8445	1	1	2	2	3	4	4	5	5
70	.8451	8457	8463	8470	8476	8482	8488	8494	8500	8506	1	1	2	2	3	4	4	5	5
71	.8513	8519	8525	8531	8537	8543	8549	8555	8561	8567	1	1	2	2	3	4	4	5	5
72	.8573	8579	8585	8591	8597	8603	8609	8615	8621	8627	1	1	2	2	3	4	4	5	5
73	.8633	8639	8645	8651	8657	8663	8669	8675	8681	8686	1	1	2	2	3	4	4	5	5
74	.8692	8698	8704	8710	8716	8722	8727	8733	8739	8745	1	1	2	2	3	4	4	5	5
75	.8751	8756	8762	8768	8774	8779	8785	8791	8797	8802	1	1	2	2	3	4	4	5	5
76	.8808	8814	8820	8825	8831	8837	8842	8848	8854	8859	1	1	2	2	3	4	4	5	5
77	.8865	8871	8876	8882	8887	8893	8899	8904	8910	8915	1	1	2	2	3	4	4	5	5
78	.8921	8927	8932	8938	8943	8949	8954	8960	8965	8971	1	1	2	2	3	4	4	5	5
79	.8976	8982	8987	8993	8998	9004	9009	9015	9020	9025	1	1	2	2	3	4	4	5	5
80	.9031	9036	9042	9047	9053	9058	9063	9069	9074	9079	1	1	2	2	3	3	4	4	5
81	.9085	9090	9096	9101	9106	9112	9117	9122	9128	9133	1	1	2	2	3	3	4	4	5
82	.9138	9143	9149	9154	9159	9165	9170	9175	9180	9186	1	1	2	2	3	3	4	4	5
83	.9191	9196	9201	9206	9212	9217	9222	9227	9232	9238	1	1	2	2	3	3	4	4	5
84	.9243	9248	9253	9258	9263	9269	9274	9279	9284	9289	1	1	2	2	3	3	4	4	5
85	.9294	9299	9304	9309	9315	9320	9325	9330	9335	9340	1	1	2	2	3	3	4	4	5
86	.9345	9350	9355	9360	9365	9370	9375	9380	9385	9390	1	1	2	2	3	3	4	4	5
87	.9395	9400	9405	9410	9415	9420	9425	9430	9435	9440	0	1	1	2	2	3	3	4	4
88	.9445	9450	9455	9460	9465	9469	9474	9479	9484	9489	0	1	1	2	2	3	3	4	4
89	.9494	9499	9504	9509	9513	9518	9523	9528	9533	9538	0	1	1	2	2	3	3	4	4
90	.9542	9547	9552	9557	9562	9566	9571	9576	9581	9586	0	1	1	2	2	3	3	4	4
91	.9590	9595	9600	9605	9609	9614	9619	9624	9628	9633	0	1	1	2	2	3	3	4	4
92	.9638	9643	9647	9652	9657	9661	9666	9671	9675	9680	0	1	1	2	2	3	3	4	4
93	.9685	9689	9694	9699	9703	9708	9713	9717	9722	9727	0	1	1	2	2	3	3	4	4
94	.9731	9736	9741	9745	9750	9754	9759	9763	9768	9773	0	1	1	2	2	3	3	4	4
95	.9777	9782	9786	9791	9795	9800	9805	9809	9814	9818	0	1	1	2	2	3	3	4	4
96	.9823	9827	9832	9836	9841	9845	9850	9854	9859	9863	0	1	1	2	2	2	3	3	4
97	.9868	9872	9877	9881	9886	9890	9894	9899	9903	9908	0	1	1	2	2	2	3	3	4
98	.9912	9917	9921	9926	9930	9934	9939	9943	9948	9952	0	1	1	2	2	2	3	3	4
99	.9956	9961	9965	9969	9974	9978	9983	9987	9991	9996	0	1	1	2	2	2	3	3	4

$$\ln x = \log_e x = \ln 10 \times \lg x \approx 2.3026 \times \lg x$$
$$\lg x = \log_{10} x = \lg e \times \ln x \approx 0.43429 \times \ln x$$

n	1	2	3	4	5	6	7	8	9	10
$\lg e^n$	0.4343	0.8686	1.3029	1.7372	2.1715	2.6058	3.0401	3.4744	3.9087	4.3429
$\lg e^{-n}$	$\bar{1}.5657$	$\bar{1}.1314$	$\bar{2}.6971$	$\bar{2}.2628$	$\bar{3}.8285$	$\bar{3}.3942$	$\bar{4}.9599$	$\bar{4}.5256$	$\bar{4}.0913$	$\bar{5}.6571$

x	0	1	2	3	4	5	6	7	8	9	1 2 3	4 5 6	7 8 9
												ADD	
.00	1000	1002	1005	1007	1009	1012	1014	1016	1019	1021	0 0 1	1 1 1	1 2 2
.01	1023	1026	1028	1030	1033	1035	1038	1040	1042	1045	0 0 1	1 1 1	1 2 2
.02	1047	1050	1052	1054	1057	1059	1062	1064	1067	1069	0 0 1	1 1 1	1 2 2
.03	1072	1074	1076	1079	1081	1084	1086	1089	1091	1094	0 1 1	1 1 1	1 2 2
.04	1096	1099	1102	1104	1107	1109	1112	1114	1117	1119	0 1 1	1 1 2	2 2 3
.05	1122	1125	1127	1130	1132	1135	1138	1140	1143	1146	0 1 1	1 1 2	2 2 3
.06	1148	1151	1153	1156	1159	1161	1164	1167	1169	1172	0 1 1	1 1 2	2 2 3
.07	1175	1178	1180	1183	1186	1189	1191	1194	1197	1199	0 1 1	1 1 2	2 2 3
.08	1202	1205	1208	1211	1213	1216	1219	1222	1225	1227	0 1 1	1 1 2	2 2 3
.09	1230	1233	1236	1239	1242	1245	1247	1250	1253	1256	0 1 1	1 1 2	2 2 3
.10	1259	1262	1265	1268	1271	1274	1276	1279	1282	1285	0 1 1	1 1 2	2 2 3
.11	1288	1291	1294	1297	1300	1303	1306	1309	1312	1315	0 1 1	1 2 2	2 2 3
.12	1318	1321	1324	1327	1330	1334	1337	1340	1343	1346	0 1 1	1 2 2	2 2 3
.13	1349	1352	1355	1358	1361	1365	1368	1371	1374	1377	0 1 1	1 2 2	2 2 3
.14	1380	1384	1387	1390	1393	1396	1400	1403	1406	1409	0 1 1	1 2 2	2 2 3
.15	1413	1416	1419	1422	1426	1429	1432	1435	1439	1442	0 1 1	1 2 2	2 2 3
.16	1445	1449	1452	1455	1459	1462	1466	1469	1472	1476	0 1 1	1 2 2	2 2 3
.17	1479	1483	1486	1489	1493	1496	1500	1503	1507	1510	0 1 1	2 2 2	3 3 4
.18	1514	1517	1521	1524	1528	1531	1535	1538	1542	1545	0 1 1	2 2 2	3 3 4
.19	1549	1552	1556	1560	1563	1567	1570	1574	1578	1581	0 1 1	2 2 2	3 3 4
.20	1585	1589	1592	1596	1600	1603	1607	1611	1614	1618	0 1 1	2 2 2	3 3 4
.21	1622	1626	1629	1633	1637	1641	1644	1648	1652	1656	0 1 1	2 2 2	3 3 4
.22	1660	1663	1667	1671	1675	1679	1683	1687	1690	1694	0 1 1	2 2 2	3 3 4
.23	1698	1702	1706	1710	1714	1718	1722	1726	1730	1734	0 1 1	2 2 2	3 3 4
.24	1738	1742	1746	1750	1754	1758	1762	1766	1770	1774	0 1 1	2 2 2	3 3 4
.25	1778	1782	1786	1791	1795	1799	1803	1807	1811	1816	0 1 1	2 2 2	3 3 4
.26	1820	1824	1828	1832	1837	1841	1845	1849	1854	1858	0 1 1	2 2 2	3 3 4
.27	1862	1866	1871	1875	1879	1884	1888	1892	1897	1901	0 1 1	2 2 2	3 3 4
.28	1905	1910	1914	1919	1923	1928	1932	1936	1941	1945	0 1 1	2 2 2	3 3 4
.29	1950	1954	1959	1963	1968	1972	1977	1982	1986	1991	0 1 1	2 2 2	3 3 4
.30	1995	2000	2004	2009	2014	2018	2023	2028	2032	2037	0 1 1	2 2 3	3 4 4
.31	2042	2046	2051	2056	2061	2065	2070	2075	2080	2084	0 1 1	2 2 3	3 4 4
.32	2089	2094	2099	2104	2109	2113	2118	2123	2128	2133	0 1 1	2 2 3	3 4 4
.33	2138	2143	2148	2153	2158	2163	2168	2173	2178	2183	1 1 2	2 3 3	4 4 5
.34	2188	2193	2198	2203	2208	2213	2218	2223	2228	2234	1 1 2	2 3 3	4 4 5
.35	2239	2244	2249	2254	2259	2265	2270	2275	2280	2286	1 1 2	2 3 3	4 4 5
.36	2291	2296	2301	2307	2312	2317	2323	2328	2333	2339	1 1 2	2 3 3	4 4 5
.37	2344	2350	2355	2360	2366	2371	2377	2382	2388	2393	1 1 2	2 3 4	4 5 5
.38	2399	2404	2410	2415	2421	2427	2432	2438	2443	2449	1 1 2	2 3 4	4 5 5
.39	2455	2460	2466	2472	2477	2483	2489	2495	2500	2506	1 1 2	2 3 4	4 5 5
.40	2512	2518	2523	2529	2535	2541	2547	2553	2559	2564	1 1 2	2 3 4	4 5 5
.41	2570	2576	2582	2588	2594	2600	2606	2612	2618	2624	1 1 2	2 3 4	4 5 5
.42	2630	2636	2642	2649	2655	2661	2667	2673	2679	2685	1 1 2	2 3 4	4 5 5
.43	2692	2698	2704	2710	2716	2723	2729	2735	2742	2748	1 1 2	2 3 4	4 5 5
.44	2754	2761	2767	2773	2780	2786	2793	2799	2805	2812	1 1 2	2 3 4	4 5 5
.45	2818	2825	2831	2838	2844	2851	2858	2864	2871	2877	1 1 2	3 3 4	5 6 6
.46	2884	2891	2897	2904	2911	2917	2924	2931	2938	2944	1 1 2	3 3 4	5 6 6
.47	2951	2958	2965	2972	2979	2985	2992	2999	3006	3013	1 1 2	3 3 4	5 6 6
.48	3020	3027	3034	3041	3048	3055	3062	3069	3076	3083	1 1 2	3 4 4	5 6 6
.49	3090	3097	3105	3112	3119	3126	3133	3141	3148	3155	1 1 2	3 4 4	5 6 6

Examples: antilog 0.5652 = 3.673 + 0.002 = 3.675
antilog 2·5652 = 3.675 × 10^2
antilog $\bar{3}$.5652 = 3.675 × 10^{-3}
antilog (-1.37) = antilog $\bar{2}$.63 = 4.266 × 10^{-2}

x	0	1	2	3	4	5	6	7	8	9	1 2 3	4 5 6	7 8 9
												ADD	
.50	3162	3170	3177	3184	3192	3199	3206	3214	3221	3228	1 1 2	3 4 4	5 6 6
.51	3236	3243	3251	3258	3266	3273	3281	3289	3296	3304	1 2 2	3 4 5	6 6 7
.52	3311	3319	3327	3334	3342	3350	3357	3365	3373	3381	1 2 2	3 4 5	6 6 7
.53	3388	3396	3404	3412	3420	3428	3436	3443	3451	3459	1 2 2	3 4 5	6 6 7
.54	3467	3475	3483	3491	3499	3508	3516	3524	3532	3540	1 2 2	3 4 5	6 6 7
.55	3548	3556	3565	3573	3581	3589	3597	3606	3614	3622	1 2 2	3 4 5	6 6 7
.56	3631	3639	3648	3656	3664	3673	3681	3690	3698	3707	1 2 2	3 4 5	6 6 7
.57	3715	3724	3733	3741	3750	3758	3767	3776	3784	3793	1 2 3	4 4 5	6 7 8
.58	3802	3811	3819	3828	3837	3846	3855	3864	3873	3882	1 2 3	4 4 5	6 7 8
.59	3890	3899	3908	3917	3926	3936	3945	3954	3963	3972	1 2 3	4 5 5	6 7 8
.60	3981	3990	3999	4009	4018	4027	4036	4046	4055	4064	1 2 3	4 5 5	6 7 8
.61	4074	4083	4093	4102	4111	4121	4130	4140	4150	4159	1 2 3	4 5 6	7 8 9
.62	4169	4178	4188	4198	4207	4217	4227	4236	4246	4256	1 2 3	4 5 6	7 8 9
.63	4266	4276	4285	4295	4305	4315	4325	4335	4345	4355	1 2 3	4 5 6	7 8 9
.64	4365	4375	4385	4395	4406	4416	4426	4436	4446	4457	1 2 3	4 5 6	7 8 9
.65	4467	4477	4487	4498	4508	4519	4529	4539	4550	4560	1 2 3	4 5 6	7 8 9
.66	4571	4581	4592	4603	4613	4624	4634	4645	4656	4667	1 2 3	4 5 7	8 9 10
.67	4677	4688	4699	4710	4721	4732	4742	4753	4764	4775	1 2 3	4 5 7	8 9 10
.68	4786	4797	4808	4819	4831	4842	4853	4864	4875	4887	1 2 3	4 6 7	8 9 10
.69	4898	4909	4920	4932	4943	4955	4966	4977	4989	5000	1 2 3	4 6 7	8 9 10
.70	5012	5023	5035	5047	5058	5070	5082	5093	5105	5117	1 2 4	5 6 7	8 10 11
.71	5129	5140	5152	5164	5176	5188	5200	5212	5224	5236	1 2 4	5 6 7	8 10 11
.72	5248	5260	5272	5284	5297	5309	5321	5333	5346	5358	1 2 4	5 6 7	8 10 11
.73	5370	5383	5395	5408	5420	5433	5445	5458	5470	5483	1 2 4	5 6 7	8 10 11
.74	5495	5508	5521	5534	5546	5559	5572	5585	5598	5610	1 3 4	5 6 8	9 10 12
.75	5623	5636	5649	5662	5675	5689	5702	5715	5728	5741	1 3 4	5 7 8	9 10 12
.76	5754	5768	5781	5794	5808	5821	5834	5848	5861	5875	1 3 4	5 7 8	9 10 12
.77	5888	5902	5916	5929	5943	5957	5970	5984	5998	6012	1 3 4	6 7 8	10 11 13
.78	6026	6039	6053	6067	6081	6095	6109	6124	6138	6152	1 3 4	6 7 8	10 11 13
.79	6166	6180	6194	6209	6223	6237	6252	6266	6281	6295	1 3 4	6 7 8	10 11 13
.80	6310	6324	6339	6353	6368	6383	6397	6412	6427	6442	1 3 4	6 7 9	10 12 13
.81	6457	6471	6486	6501	6516	6531	6546	6561	6577	6592	2 3 5	6 8 9	11 12 14
.82	6607	6622	6637	6653	6668	6683	6699	6714	6730	6745	2 3 5	6 8 9	11 12 14
.83	6761	6776	6792	6808	6823	6839	6855	6871	6887	6902	2 3 5	6 8 10	11 13 14
.84	6918	6934	6950	6966	6982	6998	7015	7031	7047	7063	2 3 5	6 8 10	11 13 14
.85	7079	7096	7112	7129	7145	7161	7178	7194	7211	7228	2 3 5	6 8 10	11 13 14
.86	7244	7261	7278	7295	7311	7328	7345	7362	7379	7396	2 3 5	7 8 10	12 14 15
.87	7413	7430	7447	7464	7482	7499	7516	7534	7551	7568	2 3 5	7 9 10	12 14 15
.88	7586	7603	7621	7638	7656	7674	7691	7709	7727	7745	2 4 5	7 9 11	13 14 16
.89	7762	7780	7798	7816	7834	7852	7870	7889	7907	7925	2 4 5	7 9 11	13 14 16
.90	7943	7962	7980	7998	8017	8035	8054	8072	8091	8110	2 4 5	7 9 11	13 14 16
.91	8128	8147	8166	8185	8204	8222	8241	8260	8279	8299	2 4 6	8 10 11	13 15 17
.92	8318	8337	8356	8375	8395	8414	8433	8453	8472	8492	2 4 6	8 10 11	13 15 17
.93	8511	8531	8551	8570	8590	8610	8630	8650	8670	8690	2 4 6	8 10 12	14 16 18
.94	8710	8730	8750	8770	8790	8810	8831	8851	8872	8892	2 4 6	8 10 12	14 16 18
.95	8913	8933	8954	8974	8995	9016	9036	9057	9078	9099	2 4 6	8 10 13	15 17 19
.96	9120	9141	9162	9183	9204	9226	9247	9268	9290	9311	2 4 6	8 11 13	15 17 19
.97	9333	9354	9376	9397	9419	9441	9462	9484	9506	9528	2 4 7	9 11 13	15 18 20
.98	9550	9572	9594	9616	9638	9661	9683	9705	9727	9750	2 4 7	9 11 13	15 18 20
.99	9772	9795	9817	9840	9863	9886	9908	9931	9954	9977	2 5 7	9 11 14	16 18 21

$$\exp x = e^x = \text{antilog}\,(x\ \lg e) \approx \text{antilog}\,(0.43429\ x)$$
$$\text{antilog}\ x = 10^x = \exp\,(x\ \ln 10) \approx \exp\,(2.3026\ x)$$

LOGARITHMS OF SINES   lg sin x°

x°	0' 0°.0	6' 0°.1	12' 0°.2	18' 0°.3	24' 0°.4	30' 0°.5	36' 0°.6	42' 0°.7	48' 0°.8	54' 0°.9
0°	−∞	$\bar{3}$.242	$\bar{3}$.543	$\bar{3}$.719	$\bar{3}$.844	$\bar{3}$.941	$\bar{2}$.020	$\bar{2}$.087	$\bar{2}$.145	$\bar{2}$.196
1	$\bar{2}$.242	$\bar{2}$.283	$\bar{2}$.321	$\bar{2}$.356	$\bar{2}$.388	$\bar{2}$.418	$\bar{2}$.446	$\bar{2}$.472	$\bar{2}$.497	$\bar{2}$.521
2	$\bar{2}$.543	$\bar{2}$.564	$\bar{2}$.584	$\bar{2}$.603	$\bar{2}$.622	$\bar{2}$.640	$\bar{2}$.657	$\bar{2}$.673	$\bar{2}$.689	$\bar{2}$.704
3	$\bar{2}$.719	$\bar{2}$.733	$\bar{2}$.747	$\bar{2}$.760	$\bar{2}$.773	$\bar{2}$.786	$\bar{2}$.798	$\bar{2}$.810	$\bar{2}$.821	$\bar{2}$.833
4	$\bar{2}$.844	$\bar{2}$.854	$\bar{2}$.865	$\bar{2}$.875	$\bar{2}$.885	$\bar{2}$.895	$\bar{2}$.904	$\bar{2}$.913	$\bar{2}$.923	$\bar{2}$.932
5	$\bar{2}$.940	$\bar{2}$.949	$\bar{2}$.957	$\bar{2}$.966	$\bar{2}$.974	$\bar{2}$.982	$\bar{2}$.989	$\bar{2}$.997	$\bar{1}$.005	$\bar{1}$.012
6	$\bar{1}$.019	1.026	1.033	1.040	1.047	1.054	1.060	1.067	1.073	1.080
7	$\bar{1}$.0859	0920	0981	1040	1099	1157	1214	1271	1326	1381
8	$\bar{1}$.1436	1489	1542	1594	1646	1697	1747	1797	1847	1895
9	$\bar{1}$.1943	1991	2038	2085	2131	2176	2221	2266	2310	2353
10	$\bar{1}$.2397	2439	2482	2524	2565	2606	2647	2687	2727	2767
11	$\bar{1}$.2806	2845	2883	2921	2959	2997	3034	3070	3107	3143
12	$\bar{1}$.3179	3214	3250	3284	3319	3353	3387	3421	3455	3488
13	$\bar{1}$.3521	3554	3586	3618	3650	3682	3713	3745	3775	3806
14	$\bar{1}$.3837	3867	3897	3927	3957	3986	4015	4044	4073	4102
15	$\bar{1}$.4130	4158	4186	4214	4242	4269	4296	4323	4350	4377
16	$\bar{1}$.4403	4430	4456	4482	4508	4533	4559	4584	4609	4634
17	$\bar{1}$.4659	4684	4709	4733	4757	4781	4805	4829	4853	4876
18	$\bar{1}$.4900	4923	4946	4969	4992	5015	5037	5060	5082	5104
19	$\bar{1}$.5126	5148	5170	5192	5213	5235	5256	5278	5299	5320
20	$\bar{1}$.5341	5361	5382	5402	5423	5443	5463	5484	5504	5523
21	$\bar{1}$.5543	5563	5583	5602	5621	5641	5660	5679	5698	5717
22	$\bar{1}$.5736	5754	5773	5792	5810	5828	5847	5865	5883	5901
23	$\bar{1}$.5919	5937	5954	5972	5990	6007	6024	6042	6059	6076
24	$\bar{1}$.6093	6110	6127	6144	6161	6177	6194	6210	6227	6243
25	$\bar{1}$.6259	6276	6292	6308	6324	6340	6356	6371	6387	6403
26	$\bar{1}$.6418	6434	6449	6465	6480	6495	6510	6526	6541	6556
27	$\bar{1}$.6570	6585	6600	6615	6629	6644	6659	6673	6687	6702
28	$\bar{1}$.6716	6730	6744	6759	6773	6787	6801	6814	6828	6842
29	$\bar{1}$.6856	6869	6883	6896	6910	6923	6937	6950	6963	6977
30	$\bar{1}$.6990	7003	7016	7029	7042	7055	7068	7080	7093	7106
31	$\bar{1}$.7118	7131	7144	7156	7168	7181	7193	7205	7218	7230
32	$\bar{1}$.7242	7254	7266	7278	7290	7302	7314	7326	7338	7349
33	$\bar{1}$.7361	7373	7384	7396	7407	7419	7430	7442	7453	7464
34	$\bar{1}$.7476	7487	7498	7509	7520	7531	7542	7553	7564	7575

ADD (1' 2' 3' 4' 5')

Interpolation is unreliable for x° < 1°

1'	2'	3'	4'	5'
3	7	10	14	17
3	6	10	13	16
3	5	8	11	13
2	4	7	9	11
2	4	6	8	10
2	3	5	7	8
2	3	5	6	8
1	3	4	5	7
1	2	3	5	6
10	20	30	41	51
10	19	29	39	48
9	18	28	37	46
9	17	26	35	43
8	16	25	33	41
8	16	24	31	39
7	15	22	29	37
7	14	21	28	35
7	13	20	27	33
6	13	19	25	32
6	12	18	24	30
6	12	18	23	29
6	11	17	23	28
5	11	16	21	27
5	10	16	21	26
5	10	15	19	24
5	9	14	18	23
4	9	13	17	22
4	8	12	16	20
4	8	11	15	19
4	7	11	15	18
3	7	10	13	17
3	6	10	13	16
3	6	9	12	15
3	6	9	11	14
3	6	8	11	14
3	5	8	11	13
3	5	8	10	13
2	5	7	10	12
2	5	7	9	12
2	4	7	9	11
2	4	6	9	11
2	4	6	8	10
2	4	6	8	10
2	4	6	8	10
2	4	6	7	9

This table gives only 3 decimal places for x° < 7°; the following gives 4.

†LOGARITHMS OF SINES OF SMALL ANGLES

For angles up to 1°:   lg sin x' = lg x + $\bar{4}$.4637

For angles up to 7°:   lg sin x° = lg x + S

x°	0°.00	1°.11	2°.40	3°.21	3°.85	4°.40	4°.89
S		$\bar{2}$.2419	$\bar{2}$.2418	$\bar{2}$.2417	$\bar{2}$.2416	$\bar{2}$.2415	$\bar{2}$.2414

x°	4°.89	5°.33	5°.74	6°.12	6°.48	6°.82	7°.14
S		$\bar{2}$.2413	$\bar{2}$.2412	$\bar{2}$.2411	$\bar{2}$.2410	$\bar{2}$.2409	$\bar{2}$.2408

$x°$	0' 0°.0	6' 0°.1	12' 0°.2	18' 0°.3	24' 0°.4	30' 0°.5	36' 0°.6	42' 0°.7	48' 0°.8	54' 0°.9	1'	2'	3'	4'	5' ADD
35	$\overline{1}.7586$	7597	7607	7618	7629	7640	7650	7661	7671	7682	2	4	5	7	9
36	$\overline{1}.7692$	7703	7713	7723	7734	7744	7754	7764	7774	7785	2	3	5	7	8
37	$\overline{1}.7795$	7805	7815	7825	7835	7844	7854	7864	7874	7884	2	3	5	7	8
38	$\overline{1}.7893$	7903	7913	7922	7932	7941	7951	7960	7970	7979	2	3	5	7	8
39	$\overline{1}.7989$	7998	8007	8017	8026	8035	8044	8053	8063	8072	2	3	5	6	8
40	$\overline{1}.8081$	8090	8099	8108	8117	8125	8134	8143	8152	8161	1	3	4	6	7
41	$\overline{1}.8169$	8178	8187	8195	8204	8213	8221	8230	8238	8247	1	3	4	6	7
42	$\overline{1}.8255$	8264	8272	8280	8289	8297	8305	8313	8322	8330	1	3	4	5	7
43	$\overline{1}.8338$	8346	8354	8362	8370	8378	8386	8394	8402	8410	1	3	4	5	7
44	$\overline{1}.8418$	8426	8433	8441	8449	8457	8464	8472	8480	8487	1	3	4	5	7
45	$\overline{1}.8495$	8502	8510	8517	8525	8532	8540	8547	8555	8562	1	2	4	5	6
46	$\overline{1}.8569$	8577	8584	8591	8598	8606	8613	8620	8627	8634	1	2	4	5	6
47	$\overline{1}.8641$	8648	8655	8662	8669	8676	8683	8690	8697	8704	1	2	4	5	6
48	$\overline{1}.8711$	8718	8724	8731	8738	8745	8751	8758	8765	8771	1	2	3	5	6
49	$\overline{1}.8778$	8784	8791	8797	8804	8810	8817	8823	8830	8836	1	2	3	4	5
50	$\overline{1}.8843$	8849	8855	8862	8868	8874	8880	8887	8893	8899	1	2	3	4	5
51	$\overline{1}.8905$	8911	8917	8923	8929	8935	8941	8947	8953	8959	1	2	3	4	5
52	$\overline{1}.8965$	8971	8977	8983	8989	8995	9000	9006	9012	9018	1	2	3	4	5
53	$\overline{1}.9023$	9029	9035	9041	9046	9052	9057	9063	9069	9074	1	2	3	4	5
54	$\overline{1}.9080$	9085	9091	9096	9101	9107	9112	9118	9123	9128	1	2	3	3	4
55	$\overline{1}.9134$	9139	9144	9149	9155	9160	9165	9170	9175	9181	1	2	3	3	4
56	$\overline{1}.9186$	9191	9196	9201	9206	9211	9216	9221	9226	9231	1	2	3	3	4
57	$\overline{1}.9236$	9241	9246	9251	9255	9260	9265	9270	9275	9279	1	2	2	3	4
58	$\overline{1}.9284$	9289	9294	9298	9303	9308	9312	9317	9322	9326	1	2	2	3	4
59	$\overline{1}.9331$	9335	9340	9344	9349	9353	9358	9362	9367	9371	1	1	2	3	3
60	$\overline{1}.9375$	9380	9384	9388	9393	9397	9401	9406	9410	9414	1	1	2	3	3
61	$\overline{1}.9418$	9422	9427	9431	9435	9439	9443	9447	9451	9455	1	1	2	3	3
62	$\overline{1}.9459$	9463	9467	9471	9475	9479	9483	9487	9491	9495	1	1	2	3	3
63	$\overline{1}.9499$	9503	9506	9510	9514	9518	9522	9525	9529	9533	1	1	2	3	3
64	$\overline{1}.9537$	9540	9544	9548	9551	9555	9558	9562	9566	9569	1	1	2	3	3
65	$\overline{1}.9573$	9576	9580	9583	9587	9590	9594	9597	9601	9604	1	1	2	2	3
66	$\overline{1}.9607$	9611	9614	9617	9621	9624	9627	9631	9634	9637	1	1	2	2	3
67	$\overline{1}.9640$	9643	9647	9650	9653	9656	9659	9662	9666	9669	1	1	2	2	3
68	$\overline{1}.9672$	9675	9678	9681	9684	9687	9690	9693	9696	9699	0	1	1	2	2
69	$\overline{1}.9702$	9704	9707	9710	9713	9716	9719	9722	9724	9727	0	1	1	2	2
70	$\overline{1}.9730$	9733	9735	9738	9741	9743	9746	9749	9751	9754	0	1	1	2	2
71	$\overline{1}.9757$	9759	9762	9764	9767	9770	9772	9775	9777	9780	0	1	1	1	2
72	$\overline{1}.9782$	9785	9787	9789	9792	9794	9797	9799	9801	9804	0	1	1	1	2
73	$\overline{1}.9806$	9808	9811	9813	9815	9817	9820	9822	9824	9826	0	1	1	1	2
74	$\overline{1}.9828$	9831	9833	9835	9837	9839	9841	9843	9845	9847	0	1	1	1	2
75	$\overline{1}.9849$	9851	9853	9855	9857	9859	9861	9863	9865	9867	0	1	1	1	2
76	$\overline{1}.9869$	9871	9873	9875	9876	9878	9880	9882	9884	9885	0	1	1	1	2
77	$\overline{1}.9887$	9889	9891	9892	9894	9896	9897	9899	9901	9902	0	1	1	1	2
78	$\overline{1}.9904$	9906	9907	9909	9910	9912	9913	9915	9916	9918	0	1	1	1	2
79	$\overline{1}.9919$	9921	9922	9924	9925	9927	9928	9929	9931	9932	0	1	1	1	2
80	$\overline{1}.9934$	9935	9936	9937	9939	9940	9941	9943	9944	9945					
81	$\overline{1}.9946$	9947	9949	9950	9951	9952	9953	9954	9955	9956					
82	$\overline{1}.9958$	9959	9960	9961	9962	9963	9964	9965	9966	9967					
83	$\overline{1}.9968$	9968	9969	9970	9971	9972	9973	9974	9975	9975					
84	$\overline{1}.9976$	9977	9978	9978	9979	9980	9981	9981	9982	9983					
85	$\overline{1}.9983$	9984	9985	9985	9986	9987	9987	9988	9988	9989					
86	$\overline{1}.9989$	9990	9990	9991	9991	9992	9992	9993	9993	9994					
87	$\overline{1}.9994$	9994	9995	9995	9996	9996	9996	9996	9997	9997					
88	$\overline{1}.9997$	9998	9998	9998	9998	9999	9999	9999	9999	9999					
89	$\overline{1}.9999$	9999	0.0000	0000	0000	0000	0000	0000	0000	0000					

lg cosec $x° = -$ lg sin $x°$

LOGARITHMS OF COSINES   lg cos x°

x°	0' 0°.0	6' 0°.1	12' 0°.2	18' 0°.3	24' 0°.4	30' 0°.5	36' 0°.6	42' 0°.7	48' 0°.8	54' 0°.9	1' 2' 3' 4' 5' SUBTRACT
0°	0.0000	0000	0000	0000	0000	0000	0000	0000	0000	$\bar{1}$.9999	
1	$\bar{1}$.9999	9999	9999	9999	9999	9999	9998	9998	9998	9998	
2	$\bar{1}$.9997	9997	9997	9996	9996	9996	9996	9995	9995	9994	
3	$\bar{1}$.9994	9994	9993	9993	9992	9992	9991	9991	9990	9990	
4	$\bar{1}$.9989	9989	9988	9988	9987	9987	9986	9985	9985	9984	
5	$\bar{1}$.9983	9983	9982	9981	9981	9980	9979	9978	9978	9977	
6	$\bar{1}$.9976	9975	9975	9974	9973	9972	9971	9970	9969	9968	
7	$\bar{1}$.9968	9967	9966	9965	9964	9963	9962	9961	9960	9959	
8	$\bar{1}$.9958	9956	9955	9954	9953	9952	9951	9950	9949	9947	
9	$\bar{1}$.9946	9945	9944	9943	9941	9940	9939	9937	9936	9935	
10	$\bar{1}$.9934	9932	9931	9929	9928	9927	9925	9924	9922	9921	0 1 1 1 2
11	$\bar{1}$.9919	9918	9916	9915	9913	9912	9910	9909	9907	9906	0 1 1 1 2
12	$\bar{1}$.9904	9902	9901	9899	9897	9896	9894	9892	9891	9889	0 1 1 1 2
13	$\bar{1}$.9887	9885	9884	9882	9880	9878	9876	9875	9873	9871	0 1 1 1 2
14	$\bar{1}$.9869	9867	9865	9863	9861	9859	9857	9855	9853	9851	0 1 1 1 2
15	$\bar{1}$.9849	9847	9845	9843	9841	9839	9837	9835	9833	9831	0 1 1 1 2
16	$\bar{1}$.9828	9826	9824	9822	9820	9817	9815	9813	9811	9808	0 1 1 1 2
17	$\bar{1}$.9806	9804	9801	9799	9797	9794	9792	9789	9787	9785	0 1 1 1 2
18	$\bar{1}$.9782	9780	9777	9775	9772	9770	9767	9764	9762	9759	0 1 1 2 2
19	$\bar{1}$.9757	9754	9751	9749	9746	9743	9741	9738	9735	9733	0 1 1 2 2
20	$\bar{1}$.9730	9727	9724	9722	9719	9716	9713	9710	9707	9704	0 1 1 2 2
21	$\bar{1}$.9702	9699	9696	9693	9690	9687	9684	9681	9678	9675	0 1 1 2 2
22	$\bar{1}$.9672	9669	9666	9662	9659	9656	9653	9650	9647	9643	1 1 2 2 3
23	$\bar{1}$.9640	9637	9634	9631	9627	9624	9621	9617	9614	9611	1 1 2 2 3
24	$\bar{1}$.9607	9604	9601	9597	9594	9590	9587	9583	9580	9576	1 1 2 2 3
25	$\bar{1}$.9573	9569	9566	9562	9558	9555	9551	9548	9544	9540	1 1 2 3 3
26	$\bar{1}$.9537	9533	9529	9525	9522	9518	9514	9510	9506	9503	1 1 2 3 3
27	$\bar{1}$.9499	9495	9491	9487	9483	9479	9475	9471	9467	9463	1 1 2 3 3
28	$\bar{1}$.9459	9455	9451	9447	9443	9439	9435	9431	9427	9422	1 1 2 3 3
29	$\bar{1}$.9418	9414	9410	9406	9401	9397	9393	9388	9384	9380	1 1 2 3 3
30	$\bar{1}$.9375	9371	9367	9362	9358	9353	9349	9344	9340	9335	1 1 2 3 3
31	$\bar{1}$.9331	9326	9322	9317	9312	9308	9303	9298	9294	9289	1 2 2 3 4
32	$\bar{1}$.9284	9279	9275	9270	9265	9260	9255	9251	9246	9241	1 2 2 3 4
33	$\bar{1}$.9236	9231	9226	9221	9216	9211	9206	9201	9196	9191	1 2 3 3 4
34	$\bar{1}$.9186	9181	9175	9170	9165	9160	9155	9149	9144	9139	1 2 3 3 4
35	$\bar{1}$.9134	9128	9123	9118	9112	9107	9101	9096	9091	9085	1 2 3 3 4
36	$\bar{1}$.9080	9074	9069	9063	9057	9052	9046	9041	9035	9029	1 2 3 4 5
37	$\bar{1}$.9023	9018	9012	9006	9000	8995	8989	8983	8977	8971	1 2 3 4 5
38	$\bar{1}$.8965	8959	8953	8947	8941	8935	8929	8923	8917	8911	1 2 3 4 5
39	$\bar{1}$.8905	8899	8893	8887	8880	8874	8868	8862	8855	8849	1 2 3 4 5
40	$\bar{1}$.8843	8836	8830	8823	8817	8810	8804	8797	8791	8784	1 2 3 4 5
41	$\bar{1}$.8778	8771	8765	8758	8751	8745	8738	8731	8724	8718	1 2 3 5 6
42	$\bar{1}$.8711	8704	8697	8690	8683	8676	8669	8662	8655	8648	1 2 3 5 6
43	$\bar{1}$.8641	8634	8627	8620	8613	8606	8598	8591	8584	8577	1 2 4 5 6
44	$\bar{1}$.8569	8562	8555	8547	8540	8532	8525	8517	8510	8502	1 2 4 5 6
45	$\bar{1}$.8495	8487	8480	8472	8464	8457	8449	8441	8433	8426	1 3 4 5 7
46	$\bar{1}$.8418	8410	8402	8394	8386	8378	8370	8362	8354	8346	1 3 4 5 7
47	$\bar{1}$.8338	8330	8322	8313	8305	8297	8289	8280	8272	8264	1 3 4 5 7
48	$\bar{1}$.8255	8247	8238	8230	8221	8213	8204	8195	8187	8178	1 3 4 6 7
49	$\bar{1}$.8169	8161	8152	8143	8134	8125	8117	8108	8099	8090	1 3 4 6 7
50	$\bar{1}$.8081	8072	8063	8053	8044	8035	8026	8017	8007	7998	2 3 5 6 8
51	$\bar{1}$.7989	7979	7970	7960	7951	7941	7932	7922	7913	7903	2 3 5 7 8
52	$\bar{1}$.7893	7884	7874	7864	7854	7844	7835	7825	7815	7805	2 3 5 7 8
53	$\bar{1}$.7795	7785	7774	7764	7754	7744	7734	7723	7713	7703	2 3 5 7 8
54	$\bar{1}$.7692	7682	7671	7661	7650	7640	7629	7618	7607	7597	2 4 5 7 9

$$\text{lg sec } x° = -\text{lg cos } x°$$

x°	0' / 0°.0	6' / 0°.1	12' / 0°.2	18' / 0°.3	24' / 0°.4	30' / 0°.5	36' / 0°.6	42' / 0°.7	48' / 0°.8	54' / 0°.9	1'	2'	3'	4'	5' SUBTRACT
55	1̄.7586	7575	7564	7553	7542	7531	7520	7509	7498	7487	2	4	6	7	9
56	1̄.7476	7464	7453	7442	7430	7419	7407	7396	7384	7373	2	4	6	8	10
57	1̄.7361	7349	7338	7326	7314	7302	7290	7278	7266	7254	2	4	6	8	10
58	1̄.7242	7230	7218	7205	7193	7181	7168	7156	7144	7131	2	4	6	8	10
59	1̄ 7118	7106	7093	7080	7068	7055	7042	7029	7016	7003	2	4	6	9	11
60	1̄.6990	6977	6963	6950	6937	6923	6910	6896	6883	6869	2	4	7	9	11
61	1̄.6856	6842	6828	6814	6801	6787	6773	6759	6744	6730	2	5	7	9	12
62	1̄.6716	6702	6687	6673	6659	6644	6629	6615	6600	6585	2	5	7	10	12
63	1̄.6570	6556	6541	6526	6510	6495	6480	6465	6449	6434	3	5	8	10	13
64	1̄.6418	6403	6387	6371	6356	6340	6324	6308	6292	6276	3	5	8	11	13
65	1̄.6259	6243	6227	6210	6194	6177	6161	6144	6127	6110	3	6	8	11	14
66	1̄.6093	6076	6059	6042	6024	6007	5990	5972	5954	5937	3	6	9	11	14
67	1̄.5919	5901	5883	5865	5847	5828	5810	5792	5773	5754	3	6	9	12	15
68	1̄.5736	5717	5698	5679	5660	5641	5621	5602	5583	5563	3	6	10	13	16
69	1̄.5543	5523	5504	5484	5463	5443	5423	5402	5382	5361	3	7	10	13	17
70	1̄.5341	5320	5299	5278	5256	5235	5213	5192	5170	5148	4	7	11	15	18
71	1̄.5126	5104	5082	5060	5037	5015	4992	4969	4946	4923	4	8	11	15	19
72	1̄.4900	4876	4853	4829	4805	4781	4757	4733	4709	4684	4	8	12	16	20
73	1̄.4659	4634	4609	4584	4559	4533	4508	4482	4456	4430	4	9	13	17	22
74	1̄.4403	4377	4350	4323	4296	4269	4242	4214	4186	4158	5	9	14	18	23
75	1̄.4130	4102	4073	4044	4015	3986	3957	3927	3897	3867	5	10	15	19	24
76	1̄.3837	3806	3775	3745	3713						5	10	16	21	26
						3682	3650	3618	3586	3554	5	11	16	21	27
77	1̄.3521	3488	3455	3421	3387						6	11	17	23	28
						3353	3319	3284	3250	3214	6	12	17	23	29
78	1̄.3179	3143	3107	3070	3034						6	12	18	24	30
						2997	2959	2921	2883	2845	6	13	19	25	32
79	1̄.2806	2767	2727	2687	2647						7	13	20	27	33
						2606	2565	2524	2482	2439	7	14	21	28	35
80	1̄.2397	2353	2310	2266	2221	2176					7	15	22	29	37
							2131	2085	2038	1991	8	16	24	31	39
81	1̄.1943	1895	1847	1797	1747						8	16	25	33	41
						1697	1646	1594	1542	1489	9	17	26	35	43
82	1̄.1436	1381	1326	1271							9	19	28	37	47
					1214	1157	1099	1040			10	19	29	39	48
									0981	0920	10	20	30	41	51
83	1̄.086	1̄.080	1̄.073	1̄.067	1̄.060	1̄.054	1̄.047	1̄.040	1̄.033	1̄.026	1	2	3	5	6
84	1̄.019	1̄.012	1̄.005	2̄.997	2̄.989	2̄.982	2̄.974	2̄.966	2̄.957	2̄.949	1	3	4	5	7
85	2̄.940	2̄.932	2̄.923	2̄.913	2̄.904						2	3	5	6	8
						2̄.895	2̄.885	2̄.875	2̄.865	2̄.854	2	3	5	7	8
86	2̄.844	2̄.833	2̄.821	2̄.810	2̄.798						2	4	6	8	10
						2̄.786	2̄.773	2̄.760	2̄.747	2̄.733	2	4	7	9	11
87	2̄.719	2̄.704	2̄.689	2̄.673	2̄.657						3	5	8	11	13
						2̄.640	2̄.622	2̄.603	2̄.584		3	6	10	13	16
										2̄.564	3	7	10	14	17
88	2̄.543	2̄.521	2̄.497	2̄.472	2̄.446	2̄.418	2̄.388	2̄.356	2̄.321	2̄.283	Interpolation is				
89	2̄.242	2̄.196	2̄.145	2̄.087	2̄.020	3̄.941	3̄.844	3̄.719	3̄.543	3̄.242	unreliable for x° > 89°				

For 4 decimal places (x° ⩾ 83°) put lg cos x° = lg sin (90° − x°) and see table †, p. 8.

MINUTES TO DECIMALS OF A DEGREE

	0'	1'	2'	3'	4'	5'	6'	7'	8'	9'
0'	0°.000	.017	.033	.050	.067	.083	.100	.117	.133	.150
10'	0°.167	.183	.200	.217	.233	.250	.267	.283	.300	.317
20'	0°.333	.350	.367	.383	.400	.417	.433	.450	.467	.483
30'	0°.500	.517	.533	.550	.567	.583	.600	.617	.633	.650
40'	0°.667	.683	.700	.717	.733	.750	.767	.783	.800	.817
50'	0°.833	.850	.867	.883	.900	.917	.933	.950	.967	.983

LOGARITHMS OF TANGENTS   lg tan $x°$

$x°$	0' 0°.0	6' 0°.1	12' 0°.2	18' 0°.3	24' 0°.4	30' 0°.5	36' 0°.6	42' 0°.7	48' 0°.8	54' 0°.9	1'	2'	3'	4'	5' ADD
0	$-\infty$	$\bar{3}$.242	$\bar{3}$.543	$\bar{3}$.719	$\bar{3}$.844	$\bar{3}$.941	$\bar{2}$.020	$\bar{2}$.087	$\bar{2}$.145	$\bar{2}$.196	Interpolation is unreliable			
1	$\bar{2}$.242	$\bar{2}$.283	$\bar{2}$.321	$\bar{2}$.356	$\bar{2}$.388	$\bar{2}$.418	$\bar{2}$.446	$\bar{2}$.472	$\bar{2}$.497	$\bar{2}$.521	for $x° < 1$			
2	$\bar{2}$.543	$\bar{2}$.564									3	7	10	14	17
			$\bar{2}$.585	$\bar{2}$.604	$\bar{2}$.622	$\bar{2}$.640	$\bar{2}$.657				3	6	9	12	15
								$\bar{2}$.674	$\bar{2}$.689	$\bar{2}$.705	3	5	8	11	13
3	$\bar{2}$.719	$\bar{2}$.734	$\bar{2}$.747	$\bar{2}$.761							2	5	7	9	12
					$\bar{2}$.774	$\bar{2}$.786	$\bar{2}$.799	$\bar{2}$.811	$\bar{2}$.822	$\bar{2}$.834	2	4	6	8	10
4	$\bar{2}$.845	$\bar{2}$.855	$\bar{2}$.866	$\bar{2}$.876	$\bar{2}$.886	$\bar{2}$.896	$\bar{2}$.906	$\bar{2}$.915	$\bar{2}$.924	$\bar{2}$.933	2	3	5	7	8
5	$\bar{2}$.942	$\bar{2}$.951	$\bar{2}$.959	$\bar{2}$.967	$\bar{2}$.976	$\bar{2}$.984	$\bar{2}$.991	$\bar{2}$.999	$\bar{1}$.007	$\bar{1}$.014	1	3	4	5	7
6	$\bar{1}$.022	$\bar{1}$.029	$\bar{1}$.036	$\bar{1}$.043	$\bar{1}$.050	$\bar{1}$.057	$\bar{1}$.063	$\bar{1}$.070	$\bar{1}$.076	$\bar{1}$.083	1	2	3	5	6
7	$\bar{1}$.0891	0954	1015								10	21	31	41	52
				1076	1135	1194	1252				10	20	29	39	49
								1310	1367	1423	9	19	28	37	47
8	$\bar{1}$.1478	1533	1587	1640							9	18	27	36	45
					1693	1745					9	17	26	35	43
							1797	1848	1898	1948	8	17	25	33	42
9	$\bar{1}$.1997	2046	2094	2142	2189						8	16	24	32	40
						2236	2282	2328	2374	2419	8	15	23	30	38
10	$\bar{1}$.2463	2507	2551	2594	2637						7	14	22	29	36
						2680	2722	2764	2805	2846	7	14	21	27	34
11	$\bar{1}$.2887	2927	2967	3006	3046						7	13	20	27	33
						3085	3123	3162	3200	3237	6	13	19	26	32
12	$\bar{1}$.3275	3312	3349	3385	3422	3458	3493	3529	3564	3599	6	12	18	24	30
13	$\bar{1}$.3634	3668	3702	3736	3770	3804	3837	3870	3903	3935	6	11	17	22	28
14	$\bar{1}$.3968	4000	4032	4064	4095	4127	4158	4189	4220	4250	5	10	16	21	26
15	$\bar{1}$.4281	4311	4341	4371	4400	4430	4459	4488	4517	4546	5	10	15	19	24
16	$\bar{1}$.4575	4603	4632	4660	4688	4716	4744	4771	4799	4826	5	9	14	19	23
17	$\bar{1}$.4853	4880	4907	4934	4961	4987	5014	5040	5066	5092	4	9	13	17	22
18	$\bar{1}$.5118	5143	5169	5195	5220	5245	5270	5295	5320	5345	4	8	13	17	21
19	$\bar{1}$.5370	5394	5419	5443	5467	5491	5516	5539	5563	5587	4	8	12	16	20
20	$\bar{1}$.5611	5634	5658	5681	5704	5727	5750	5773	5796	5819	4	8	12	15	19
21	$\bar{1}$.5842	5864	5887	5909	5932	5954	5976	5998	6020	6042	4	7	11	15	18
22	$\bar{1}$.6064	6086	6108	6129	6151	6172	6194	6215	6236	6257	4	7	11	15	18
23	$\bar{1}$.6279	6300	6321	6341	6362	6383	6404	6424	6445	6465	3	7	10	14	17
24	$\bar{1}$.6486	6506	6527	6547	6567	6587	6607	6627	6647	6667	3	7	10	13	17
25	$\bar{1}$.6687	6706	6726	6746	6765	6785	6804	6824	6843	6863	3	7	10	13	17
26	$\bar{1}$.6882	6901	6920	6939	6958	6977	6996	7015	7034	7053	3	6	10	13	16
27	$\bar{1}$.7072	7090	7109	7128	7146	7165	7183	7202	7220	7238	3	6	9	12	15
28	$\bar{1}$.7257	7275	7293	7311	7330	7348	7366	7384	7402	7420	3	6	9	12	15
29	$\bar{1}$.7438	7455	7473	7491	7509	7526	7544	7562	7579	7597	3	6	9	12	15
30	$\bar{1}$.7614	7632	7649	7667	7684	7701	7719	7736	7753	7771	3	6	9	11	14
31	$\bar{1}$.7788	7805	7822	7839	7856	7873	7890	7907	7924	7941	3	6	9	11	14
32	$\bar{1}$.7958	7975	7992	8008	8025	8042	8059	8075	8092	8109	3	6	8	11	14
33	$\bar{1}$.8125	8142	8158	8175	8191	8208	8224	8241	8257	8274	3	5	8	11	13
34	$\bar{1}$.8290	8306	8323	8339	8355	8371	8388	8404	8420	8436	3	5	8	11	13
35	$\bar{1}$.8452	8468	8484	8501	8517	8533	8549	8565	8581	8597	3	5	8	11	13
36	$\bar{1}$.8613	8629	8644	8660	8676	8692	8708	8724	8740	8755	3	5	8	11	13
37	$\bar{1}$.8771	8787	8803	8818	8834	8850	8865	8881	8897	8912	3	5	8	11	13
38	$\bar{1}$.8928	8944	8959	8975	8990	9006	9022	9037	9053	9068	3	5	8	11	13
39	$\bar{1}$.9084	9099	9115	9130	9146	9161	9176	9192	9207	9223	3	5	8	10	13
40	$\bar{1}$.9238	9254	9269	9284	9300	9315	9330	9346	9361	9376	3	5	8	10	13
41	$\bar{1}$.9392	9407	9422	9438	9453	9468	9483	9499	9514	9529	3	5	8	10	13
42	$\bar{1}$.9544	9560	9575	9590	9605	9621	9636	9651	9666	9681	3	5	8	10	13
43	$\bar{1}$.9697	9712	9727	9742	9757	9772	9788	9803	9818	9833	3	5	8	10	13
44	$\bar{1}$.9848	9864	9879	9894	9909	9924	9939	9955	9970	9985	3	5	8	10	13

For 4 decimal places ($x° < 7°$) see table ‡, p. 15.

$$\text{lg cot } x° = \text{lg tan } (90° - x) = -\text{lg tan } x°$$

[12]

x°	0' 0°.0	6' 0°.1	12' 0°.2	18' 0°.3	24' 0°.4	30' 0°.5	36' 0°.6	42' 0°.7	48' 0°.8	54' 0°.9	1'	2'	3'	4'	5' ADD
45°	0.0000	0015	0030	0045	0061	0076	0091	0106	0121	0136	3	5	8	10	13
46	0.0152	0167	0182	0197	0212	0228	0243	0258	0273	0288	3	5	8	10	13
47	0.0303	0319	0334	0349	0364	0379	0395	0410	0425	0440	3	5	8	10	13
48	0.0456	0471	0486	0501	0517	0532	0547	0562	0578	0593	3	5	8	10	13
49	0.0608	0624	0639	0654	0670	0685	0700	0716	0731	0746	3	5	8	10	13
50	0.0762	0777	0793	0808	0824	0839	0854	0870	0885	0901	3	5	8	10	13
51	0.0916	0932	0947	0963	0978	0994	1010	1025	1041	1056	3	5	8	11	13
52	0.1072	1088	1103	1119	1135	1150	1166	1182	1197	1213	3	5	8	11	13
53	0.1229	1245	1260	1276	1292	1308	1324	1340	1356	1371	3	5	8	11	13
54	0.1387	1403	1419	1435	1451	1467	1483	1499	1516	1532	3	5	8	11	13
55	0.1548	1564	1580	1596	1612	1629	1645	1661	1677	1694	3	5	8	11	13
56	0.1710	1726	1743	1759	1776	1792	1809	1825	1842	1858	3	5	8	11	13
57	0.1875	1891	1908	1925	1941	1958	1975	1992	2008	2025	3	6	8	11	14
58	0.2042	2059	2076	2093	2110	2127	2144	2161	2178	2195	3	6	9	11	14
59	0.2212	2229	2247	2264	2281	2299	2316	2333	2351	2368	3	6	9	11	14
60	0.2386	2403	2421	2438	2456	2474	2491	2509	2527	2545	3	6	9	12	15
61	0.2562	2580	2598	2616	2634	2652	2670	2689	2707	2725	3	6	9	12	15
62	0.2743	2762	2780	2798	2817	2835	2854	2872	2891	2910	3	6	9	12	15
63	0.2928	2947	2966	2985	3004	3023	3042	3061	3080	3099	3	6	10	13	16
64	0.3118	3137	3157	3176	3196	3215	3235	3254	3274	3294	3	7	10	13	17
65	0.3313	3333	3353	3373	3393	3413	3433	3453	3473	3494	3	7	10	13	17
66	0.3514	3535	3555	3576	3596	3617	3638	3659	3679	3700	3	7	10	14	17
67	0.3721	3743	3764	3785	3806	3828	3849	3871	3892	3914	4	7	11	15	18
68	0.3936	3958	3980	4002	4024	4046	4068	4091	4113	4136	4	7	11	15	18
69	0.4158	4181	4204	4227	4250	4273	4296	4319	4342	4366	4	8	12	15	19
70	0.4389	4413	4437	4461	4484	4509	4533	4557	4581	4606	4	8	12	16	20
71	0.4630	4655	4680	4705	4730	4755	4780	4805	4831	4857	4	8	13	17	21
72	0.4882	4908	4934	4960	4986	5013	5039	5066	5093	5120	4	9	13	17	22
73	0.5147	5174	5201	5229	5256	5284	5312	5340	5368	5397	5	9	14	19	23
74	0.5425	5454	5483	5512	5541	5570	5600	5629	5659	5689	5	10	15	19	24
75	0.5719	5750	5780	5811	5842	5873	5905	5936	5968	6000	5	10	16	21	26
76	0.6032	6065	6097	6130	6163	6196	6230	6264	6298	6332	6	11	17	22	28
77	0.6366	6401	6436	6471	6507	6542	6578	6615	6651	6688	6	12	18	24	30
78	0.6725	6763	6800	6838	6877						6	13	19	25	32
						6915	6954	6994	7033	7073	7	13	20	26	33
79	0.7113	7154	7195	7236	7278						7	14	21	27	34
						7320	7363	7406	7449	7493	7	14	22	29	36
80	0.7537	7581	7626	7672	7718						8	15	23	30	38
						7764	7811	7858	7906	7954	8	16	24	32	40
81	0.8003	8052	8102	8152							8	17		33	42
					8203	8255					9	17	26	35	43
							8307	8360	8413	8467	9	18	27	36	45
82	0.8522	8577	8633								9	19	28	37	47
				8690	8748	8806	8865				10	20	29	39	49
								8924	8985	9046	10	21	31	41	52
83	0.911	0.917	0.924	0.930	0.937	0.943	0.950	0.957	0.964	0.971	1	2	3	5	6
84	0.978	0.986	0.993	1.001	1.009	1.016	1.024	1.033	1.041	1.049	1	3	4	5	7
85	1.058	1.067	1.076	1.085	1.094	1.104	1.114	1.124	1.134	1.145	2	3	5	7	8
86	1.155	1.166	1.178	1.189	1.201	1.214					2	4	6	8	10
							1.226	1.239	1.253	1.266	2	5	7	9	12
87	1.281	1.295	1.311								3	5	8	10	13
				1.326	1.343	1.360	1.378	1.396			3	6	9	12	15
									1.415	1.436	3	7	10	14	17
88	1.457	1.479	1.503	1.528	1.554	1.582	1.612	1.644	1.679	1.717	Interpolation				
89	1.758	1.804	1.855	1.913	1.980	2.059	2.156	2.281	2.457	2.758	is unreliable for x° > 89°				

For 4 decimal places (x° ⩾ 83°) put lg tan x° = −lg tan (90° − x°) and see table ‡, p. 15.

x°	0' 0°.0	6' 0°.1	12' 0°.2	18' 0°.3	24' 0°.4	30' 0°.5	36' 0°.6	42' 0°.7	48' 0°.8	54' 0°.9	1'	2'	3'	4'	5' ADD
0°	0.0000	0017	0035	0052	0070	0087	0105	0122	0140	0157	3	6	9	12	15
1	0.0175	0192	0209	0227	0244	0262	0279	0297	0314	0332	3	6	9	11	14
2	0.0349	0366	0384	0401	0419	0436	0454	0471	0488	0506	3	6	9	11	14
3	0.0523	0541	0558	0576	0593	0610	0628	0645	0663	0680	3	6	9	11	14
4	0.0698	0715	0732	0750	0767	0785	0802	0819	0837	0854	3	6	9	11	14
5	0.0872	0889	0906	0924	0941	0958	0976	0993	1011	1028	3	6	9	11	14
6	0.1045	1063	1080	1097	1115	1132	1149	1167	1184	1201	3	6	9	11	14
7	0.1219	1236	1253	1271	1288	1305	1323	1340	1357	1374	3	6	9	11	14
8	0.1392	1409	1426	1444	1461	1478	1495	1513	1530	1547	3	6	9	11	14
9	0.1564	1582	1599	1616	1633	1650	1668	1685	1702	1719	3	6	9	11	14
10	0.1736	1754	1771	1788	1805	1822	1840	1857	1874	1891	3	6	9	11	14
11	0.1908	1925	1942	1959	1977	1994	2011	2028	2045	2062	3	6	9	11	14
12	0.2079	2096	2113	2130	2147	2164	2181	2198	2215	2233	3	6	9	11	14
13	0.2250	2267	2284	2300	2317	2334	2351	2368	2385	2402	3	6	8	11	14
14	0.2419	2436	2453	2470	2487	2504	2521	2538	2554	2571	3	6	8	11	14
15	0.2588	2605	2622	2639	2656	2672	2689	2706	2723	2740	3	6	8	11	14
16	0.2756	2773	2790	2807	2823	2840	2857	2874	2890	2907	3	6	8	11	14
17	0.2924	2940	2957	2974	2990	3007	3024	3040	3057	3074	3	6	8	11	14
18	0.3090	3107	3123	3140	3156	3173	3190	3206	3223	3239	3	6	8	11	14
19	0.3256	3272	3289	3305	3322	3338	3355	3371	3387	3404	3	5	8	11	13
20	0.3420	3437	3453	3469	3486	3502	3518	3535	3551	3567	3	5	8	11	13
21	0.3584	3600	3616	3633	3649	3665	3681	3697	3714	3730	3	5	8	11	13
22	0.3746	3762	3778	3795	3811	3827	3843	3859	3875	3891	3	5	8	11	13
23	0.3907	3923	3939	3955	3971	3987	4003	4019	4035	4051	3	5	8	11	13
24	0.4067	4083	4099	4115	4131	4147	4163	4179	4195	4210	3	5	8	11	13
25	0.4226	4242	4258	4274	4289	4305	4321	4337	4352	4368	3	5	8	11	13
26	0.4384	4399	4415	4431	4446	4462	4478	4493	4509	4524	3	5	8	11	13
27	0.4540	4555	4571	4586	4602	4617	4633	4648	4664	4679	3	5	8	11	13
28	0.4695	4710	4726	4741	4756	4772	4787	4802	4818	4833	3	5	8	10	13
29	0.4848	4863	4879	4894	4909	4924	4939	4955	4970	4985	3	5	8	10	13
30	0.5000	5015	5030	5045	5060	5075	5090	5105	5120	5135	3	5	8	10	13
31	0.5150	5165	5180	5195	5210	5225	5240	5255	5270	5284	2	5	7	10	12
32	0.5299	5314	5329	5344	5358	5373	5388	5402	5417	5432	2	5	7	10	12
33	0.5446	5461	5476	5490	5505	5519	5534	5548	5563	5577	2	5	7	10	12
34	0.5592	5606	5621	5635	5650	5664	5678	5693	5707	5721	2	5	7	9	12
35	0.5736	5750	5764	5779	5793	5807	5821	5835	5850	5864	2	5	7	9	12
36	0.5878	5892	5906	5920	5934	5948	5962	5976	5990	6004	2	5	7	9	12
37	0.6018	6032	6046	6060	6074	6088	6101	6115	6129	6143	2	5	7	9	12
38	0.6157	6170	6184	6198	6211	6225	6239	6252	6266	6280	2	5	7	9	12
39	0.6293	6307	6320	6334	6347	6361	6374	6388	6401	6414	2	5	7	9	12
40	0.6428	6441	6455	6468	6481	6494	6508	6521	6534	6547	2	4	7	9	11
41	0.6561	6574	6587	6600	6613	6626	6639	6652	6665	6678	2	4	7	9	11
42	0.6691	6704	6717	6730	6743	6756	6769	6782	6794	6807	2	4	6	9	11
43	0.6820	6833	6845	6858	6871	6884	6896	6909	6921	6934	2	4	6	9	11
44	0.6947	6959	6972	6984	6997	7009	7022	7034	7046	7059	2	4	6	8	10
45	0.7071	7083	7096	7108	7120	7133	7145	7157	7169	7181	2	4	6	8	10
46	0.7193	7206	7218	7230	7242	7254	7266	7278	7290	7302	2	4	6	8	10
47	0.7314	7325	7337	7349	7361	7373	7385	7396	7408	7420	2	4	6	8	10
48	0.7431	7443	7455	7466	7478	7490	7501	7513	7524	7536	2	4	6	8	10
49	0.7547	7559	7570	7581	7593	7604	7615	7627	7638	7649	2	4	6	7	9
50	0.7660	7672	7683	7694	7705	7716	7727	7738	7749	7760	2	4	6	7	9
51	0.7771	7782	7793	7804	7815	7826	7837	7848	7859	7869	2	4	5	7	9
52	0.7880	7891	7902	7912	7923	7934	7944	7955	7965	7976	2	4	5	7	9
53	0.7986	7997	8007	8018	8028	8039	8049	8059	8070	8080	2	3	5	7	8
54	0.8090	8100	8111	8121	8131	8141	8151	8161	8171	8181	2	3	5	7	8

For 4 significant figures (for small angles) use table †, p. 8, to calculate lg sin x°.

SINES sin x°

x°	0' 0°.0	6' 0°.1	12' 0°.2	18' 0°.3	24' 0°.4	30' 0°.5	36' 0°.6	42' 0°.7	48' 0°.8	54' 0°.9	1'	2'	3'	4'	5' ADD
55°	0.8192	8202	8211	8221	8231	8241	8251	8261	8271	8281	2	3	5	7	8
56	0.8290	8300	8310	8320	8329	8339	8348	8358	8368	8377	2	3	5	7	8
57	0.8387	8396	8406	8415	8425	8434	8443	8453	8462	8471	2	3	5	6	8
58	0.8480	8490	8499	8508	8517	8526	8536	8545	8554	8563	2	3	5	6	8
59	0.8572	8581	8590	8599	8607	8616	8625	8634	8643	8652	1	3	4	6	7
60	0.8660	8669	8678	8686	8695	8704	8712	8721	8729	8738	1	3	4	6	7
61	0.8746	8755	8763	8771	8780	8788	8796	8805	8813	8821	1	3	4	5	7
62	0.8829	8838	8846	8854	8862	8870	8878	8886	8894	8902	1	3	4	5	7
63	0.8910	8918	8926	8934	8942	8949	8957	8965	8973	8980	1	3	4	5	7
64	0.8988	8996	9003	9011	9018	9026	9033	9041	9048	9056	1	3	4	5	7
65	0.9063	9070	9078	9085	9092	9100	9107	9114	9121	9128	1	2	4	5	6
66	0.9135	9143	9150	9157	9164	9171	9178	9184	9191	9198	1	2	4	5	6
67	0.9205	9212	9219	9225	9232	9239	9245	9252	9259	9265	1	2	3	5	6
68	0.9272	9278	9285	9291	9298	9304	9311	9317	9323	9330	1	2	3	4	5
69	0.9336	9342	9348	9354	9361	9367	9373	9379	9385	9391	1	2	3	4	5
70	0.9397	9403	9409	9415	9421	9426	9432	9438	9444	9449	1	2	3	4	5
71	0.9455	9461	9466	9472	9478	9483	9489	9494	9500	9505	1	2	3	4	5
72	0.9511	9516	9521	9527	9532	9537	9542	9548	9553	9558	1	2	3	3	4
73	0.9563	9568	9573	9578	9583	9588	9593	9598	9603	9608	1	2	3	3	4
74	0.9613	9617	9622	9627	9632	9636	9641	9646	9650	9655	1	2	2	3	4
75	0.9659	9664	9668	9673	9677	9681	9686	9690	9694	9699	1	1	2	3	3
76	0.9703	9707	9711	9715	9720	9724	9728	9732	9736	9740	1	1	2	3	3
77	0.9744	9748	9751	9755	9759	9763	9767	9770	9774	9778	1	1	2	3	3
78	0.9781	9785	9789	9792	9796	9799	9803	9806	9810	9813	1	1	2	3	3
79	0.9816	9820	9823	9826	9829	9833	9836	9839	9842	9845	1	1	2	2	3
80	0.9848	9851	9854	9857	9860	9863	9866	9869	9871	9874	0	1	1	2	2
81	0.9877	9880	9882	9885	9888	9890	9893	9895	9898	9900	0	1	1	2	2
82	0.9903	9905	9907	9910	9912	9914	9917	9919	9921	9923	0	1	1	1	2
83	0.9925	9928	9930	9932	9934	9936	9938	9940	9942	9943	0	1	1	1	2
84	0.9945	9947	9949	9951	9952	9954	9956	9957	9959	9960	0	1	1	1	2
85	0.9962	9963	9965	9966	9968	9969	9971	9972	9973	9974					
86	0.9976	9977	9978	9979	9980	9981	9982	9983	9984	9985					
87	0.9986	9987	9988	9989	9990	9990	9991	9992	9993	9993					
88	0.9994	9995	9995	9996	9996	9997	9997	9997	9998	9998					
89	0.9998	9999	9999	9999	9999	1.000	1.000	1.000	1.000	1.000					

‡LOGARITHMS OF TANGENTS OF SMALL ANGLES

For angles up to 1°:   lg tan x' ≈ lg x + $\bar{4}$.4637
For angles up to 7°:   lg tan x° = lg x + T

x°	0°.00	1°.28	1°.97	2°.48	2°.90	3°.27	3°.60	3°.90	4°.18
T	$\bar{2}$.2419	$\bar{2}$.2420	$\bar{2}$.2421	$\bar{2}$.2422	$\bar{2}$.2423	$\bar{2}$.2424	$\bar{2}$.2425	$\bar{2}$.2426	

x°	4°.18	4°.44	4°.69	4°.92	5°.15	5°.36	5°.57	5°.77
T	$\bar{2}$.2427	$\bar{2}$.2428	$\bar{2}$.2429	$\bar{2}$.2430	$\bar{2}$.2431	$\bar{2}$.2432	$\bar{2}$.2433	

x°	5°.77	5°.96	6°.15	6°.33	6°.50	6°.67	6°.84	7°.00
T	$\bar{2}$.2434	$\bar{2}$.2435	$\bar{2}$.2436	$\bar{2}$.2437	$\bar{2}$.2438	$\bar{2}$.2439	$\bar{2}$.2440	

Example: to find lg tan 5°.20. Since 5°.20 lies between 5°.15 and 5°.36 the appropriate value of T is $\bar{2}$.2431. So lg tan 5°.20 = 0.7160 + $\bar{2}$.2431 or $\bar{2}$.9591 to 4 decimal places.

x°	0' 0°.0	6' 0°.1	12' 0°.2	18' 0°.3	24' 0°.4	30' 0°.5	36' 0°.6	42' 0°.7	48' 0°.8	54' 0°.9	1'	2'	3'	4'	5' SUBTRACT
0°	1.0000	1.000	1.000	1.000	1.000	1.000	0.9999	9999	9999	9999					
1	0.9998	9998	9998	9997	9997	9997	9996	9996	9995	9995					
2	0.9994	9993	9993	9992	9991	9990	9990	9989	9988	9987					
3	0.9986	9985	9984	9983	9982	9981	9980	9979	9978	9977					
4	0.9976	9974	9973	9972	9971	9969	9968	9966	9965	9963					
5	0.9962	9960	9959	9957	9956	9954	9952	9951	9949	9947	0	1	1	1	2
6	0.9945	9943	9942	9940	9938	9936	9934	9932	9930	9928	0	1	1	1	2
7	0.9925	9923	9921	9919	9917	9914	9912	9910	9907	9905	0	1	1	1	2
8	0.9903	9900	9898	9895	9893	9890	9888	9885	9882	9880	0	1	1	2	2
9	0.9877	9874	9871	9869	9866	9863	9860	9857	9854	9851	0	1	1	2	2
10	0.9848	9845	9842	9839	9836	9833	9829	9826	9823	9820	1	1	2	2	3
11	0.9816	9813	9810	9806	9803	9799	9796	9792	9789	9785	1	1	2	3	3
12	0.9781	9778	9774	9770	9767	9763	9759	9755	9751	9748	1	1	2	3	3
13	0.9744	9740	9736	9732	9728	9724	9720	9715	9711	9707	1	1	2	3	3
14	0.9703	9699	9694	9690	9686	9681	9677	9673	9668	9664	1	1	2	3	3
15	0.9659	9655	9650	9646	9641	9636	9632	9627	9622	9617	1	2	2	3	4
16	0.9613	9608	9603	9598	9593	9588	9583	9578	9573	9568	1	2	3	3	4
17	0.9563	9558	9553	9548	9542	9537	9532	9527	9521	9516	1	2	3	4	5
18	0.9511	9505	9500	9494	9489	9483	9478	9472	9466	9461	1	2	3	4	5
19	0.9455	9449	9444	9438	9432	9426	9421	9415	9409	9403	1	2	3	4	5
20	0.9397	9391	9385	9379	9373	9367	9361	9354	9348	9342	1	2	3	4	5
21	0.9336	9330	9323	9317	9311	9304	9298	9291	9285	9278	1	2	3	4	5
22	0.9272	9265	9259	9252	9245	9239	9232	9225	9219	9212	1	2	3	5	6
23	0.9205	9198	9191	9184	9178	9171	9164	9157	9150	9143	1	2	4	5	6
24	0.9135	9128	9121	9114	9107	9100	9092	9085	9078	9070	1	2	4	5	6
25	0.9063	9056	9048	9041	9033	9026	9018	9011	9003	8996	1	3	4	5	7
26	0.8988	8980	8973	8965	8957	8949	8942	8934	8926	8918	1	3	4	5	7
27	0.8910	8902	8894	8886	8878	8870	8862	8854	8846	8838	1	3	4	5	7
28	0.8829	8821	8813	8805	8796	8788	8780	8771	8763	8755	1	3	4	5	7
29	0.8746	8738	8729	8721	8712	8704	8695	8686	8678	8669	1	3	4	6	7
30	0.8660	8652	8643	8634	8625	8616	8607	8599	8590	8581	1	3	4	6	7
31	0.8572	8563	8554	8545	8536	8526	8517	8508	8499	8490	2	3	5	6	8
32	0.8480	8471	8462	8453	8443	8434	8425	8415	8406	8396	2	3	5	6	8
33	0.8387	8377	8368	8358	8348	8339	8329	8320	8310	8300	2	3	5	7	8
34	0.8290	8281	8271	8261	8251	8241	8231	8221	8211	8202	2	3	5	7	8

PROPORTIONAL PARTS FOR SIXTHS

Δ	1	2	3	4	5	Δ	1	2	3	4	5	Δ	1	2	3	4	5	Δ	1	2	3	4	5
1	0	0	1	1	1	16	3	5	8	11	13	31	5	10	16	21	26	46	8	15	23	31	38
2	0	1	1	1	2	17	3	6	9	11	14	32	5	11	16	21	27	47	8	16	24	31	39
3	1	1	2	2	3	18	3	6	9	12	15	33	6	11	17	22	28	48	8	16	24	32	40
4	1	1	2	3	3	19	3	6	10	13	16	34	6	11	17	23	28	49	8	16	25	33	41
5	1	2	3	3	4	20	3	7	10	13	17	35	6	12	18	23	29	50	8	17	25	33	42
6	1	2	3	4	5	21	4	7	11	14	18	36	6	12	18	24	30	51	9	17	26	34	43
7	1	2	4	5	6	22	4	7	11	15	18	37	6	12	19	25	31	52	9	17	26	35	43
8	1	3	4	5	7	23	4	8	12	15	19	38	6	13	19	25	32	53	9	18	27	35	44
9	2	3	5	6	8	24	4	8	12	16	20	39	7	13	20	26	33	54	9	18	27	36	45
10	2	3	5	7	8	25	4	8	13	17	21	40	7	13	20	27	33	55	9	18	28	37	46
11	2	4	6	7	9	26	4	9	13	17	22	41	7	14	21	27	34	56	9	19	28	37	47
12	2	4	6	8	10	27	5	9	14	18	23	42	7	14	21	28	35	57	10	19	29	38	48
13	2	4	7	9	11	28	5	9	14	19	23	43	7	14	22	29	36	58	10	19	29	39	48
14	2	5	7	9	12	29	5	10	15	19	24	44	7	15	22	29	37	59	10	20	30	39	49
15	3	5	8	10	13	30	5	10	15	20	25	45	8	15	23	30	38	60	10	20	30	40	50

COSINES cos $x°$

$x°$	0' 0°.0	6' 0°.1	12' 0°.2	18' 0°.3	24' 0°.4	30' 0°.5	36' 0°.6	42' 0°.7	48' 0°.8	54' 0°.9	1'	2'	3'	4'	5'
													SUBTRACT		
35	0.8192	8181	8171	8161	8151	8141	8131	8121	8111	8100	2	3	5	7	8
36	0.8090	8080	8070	8059	8049	8039	8028	8018	8007	7997	2	3	5	7	8
37	0.7986	7976	7965	7955	7944	7934	7923	7912	7902	7891	2	4	5	7	9
38	0.788b	7869	7859	7848	7837	7826	7815	7804	7793	7782	2	4	5	7	9
39	0.7771	7760	7749	7738	7727	7716	7705	7694	7683	7672	2	4	6	7	9
40	0.7660	7649	7638	7627	7615	7604	7593	7581	7570	7559	2	4	6	7	9
41	0.7547	7536	7524	7513	7501	7490	7478	7466	7455	7443	2	4	6	8	10
42	0.7431	7420	7408	7396	7385	7373	7361	7349	7337	7325	2	4	6	8	10
43	0.7314	7302	7290	7278	7266	7254	7242	7230	7218	7206	2	4	6	8	10
44	0.7193	7181	7169	7157	7145	7133	7120	7108	7096	7083	2	4	6	8	10
45	0.7071	7059	7046	7034	7022	7009	6997	6984	6972	6959	2	4	6	8	10
46	0.6947	6934	6921	6909	6896	6884	6871	6858	6845	6833	2	4	6	9	11
47	0.6820	6807	6794	6782	6769	6756	6743	6730	6717	6704	2	4	6	9	11
48	0.6691	6678	6665	6652	6639	6626	6613	6600	6587	6574	2	4	7	9	11
49	0.6561	6547	6534	6521	6508	6494	6481	6468	6455	6441	2	4	7	9	11
50	0.6428	6414	6401	6388	6374	6361	6347	6334	6320	6307	2	5	7	9	12
51	0.6293	6280	6266	6252	6239	6225	6211	6198	6184	6170	2	5	7	9	12
52	0.6157	6143	6129	6115	6101	6088	6074	6060	6046	6032	2	5	7	9	12
53	0.6018	6004	5990	5976	5962	5948	5934	5920	5906	5892	2	5	7	9	12
54	0.5878	5864	5850	5835	5821	5807	5793	5779	5764	5750	2	5	7	9	12
55	0.5736	5721	5707	5693	5678	5664	5650	5635	5621	5606	2	5	7	9	12
56	0.5592	5577	5563	5548	5534	5519	5505	5490	5476	5461	2	5	7	10	12
57	0.5446	5432	5417	5402	5388	5373	5358	5344	5329	5314	2	5	7	10	12
58	0.5299	5284	5270	5255	5240	5225	5210	5195	5180	5165	2	5	7	10	12
59	0.5150	5135	5120	5105	5090	5075	5060	5045	5030	5015	3	5	8	10	13
60	0.5000	4985	4970	4955	4939	4924	4909	4894	4879	4863	3	5	8	10	13
61	0.4848	4833	4818	4802	4787	4772	4756	4741	4726	4710	3	5	8	10	13
62	0.4695	4679	4664	4648	4633	4617	4602	4586	4571	4555	3	5	8	11	13
63	0.4540	4524	4509	4493	4478	4462	4446	4431	4415	4399	3	5	8	11	13
64	0.4384	4368	4352	4337	4321	4305	4289	4274	4258	4242	3	5	8	11	13
65	0.4226	4210	4195	4179	4163	4147	4131	4115	4099	4083	3	5	8	11	13
66	0.4067	4051	4035	4019	4003	3987	3971	3955	3939	3923	3	5	8	11	13
67	0.3907	3891	3875	3859	3843	3827	3811	3795	3778	3762	3	5	8	11	13
68	0.3746	3730	3714	3697	3681	3665	3649	3633	3616	3600	3	5	8	11	13
69	0.3584	3567	3551	3535	3518	3502	3486	3469	3453	3437	3	5	8	11	13
70	0.3420	3404	3387	3371	3355	3338	3322	3305	3289	3272	3	5	8	11	13
71	0.3256	3239	3223	3206	3190	3173	3156	3140	3123	3107	3	6	8	11	14
72	0.3090	3074	3057	3040	3024	3007	2990	2974	2957	2940	3	6	8	11	14
73	0.2924	2907	2890	2874	2857	2840	2823	2807	2790	2773	3	6	8	11	14
74	0.2756	2740	2723	2706	2689	2672	2656	2639	2622	2605	3	6	8	11	14
75	0.2588	2571	2554	2538	2521	2504	2487	2470	2453	2436	3	6	8	11	14
76	0.2419	2402	2385	2368	2351	2334	2317	2300	2284	2267	3	6	8	11	14
77	0.2250	2233	2215	2198	2181	2164	2147	2130	2113	2096	3	6	9	11	14
78	0.2079	2062	2045	2028	2011	1994	1977	1959	1942	1925	3	6	9	11	14
79	0.1908	1891	1874	1857	1840	1822	1805	1788	1771	1754	3	6	9	11	14
80	0.1736	1719	1702	1685	1668	1650	1633	1616	1599	1582	3	6	9	11	14
81	0.1564	1547	1530	1513	1495	1478	1461	1444	1426	1409	3	6	9	11	14
82	0.1392	1374	1357	1340	1323	1305	1288	1271	1253	1236	3	6	9	11	14
83	0.1219	1201	1184	1167	1149	1132	1115	1097	1080	1063	3	6	9	11	14
84	0.1045	1028	1011	0993	0976	0958	0941	0924	0906	0889	3	6	9	11	14
85	0.0872	0854	0837	0819	0802	0785	0767	0750	0732	0715	3	6	9	11	14
86	0.0698	0680	0663	0645	0628	0610	0593	0576	0558	0541	3	6	9	11	14
87	0.0523	0506	0488	0471	0454	0436	0419	0401	0384	0366	3	6	9	11	14
88	0.0349	0332	0314	0297	0279	0262	0244	0227	0209	0192	3	6	9	11	14
89	0.0175	0157	0140	0122	0105	0087	0070	0052	0035	0017	3	6	9	12	15

For 4 significant figures (for angles near 90°) put cos $x°$ = sin $(90° - x°)$ and use table †, p. 8.

[17]

TANGENTS   tan x°

x°	0' 0°.0	6' 0°.1	12' 0°.2	18' 0°.3	24' 0'.4	30' 0°.5	36' 0°.6	42' 0°.7	48' 0°.8	54' 0°.9	1'	2'	3'	4'	5' ADD
0°	0.0000	0017	0035	0052	0070	0087	0105	0122	0140	0157	3	6	9	11	14
1	0.0175	0192	0209	0227	0244	0262	0279	0297	0314	0332	3	6	9	11	14
2	0.0349	0367	0384	0402	0419	0437	0454	0472	0489	0507	3	6	9	12	15
3	0.0524	0542	0559	0577	0594	0612	0629	0647	0664	0682	3	6	9	12	15
4	0.0699	0717	0734	0752	0769	0787	0805	0822	0840	0857	3	6	9	12	15
5	0.0875	0892	0910	0928	0945	0963	0981	0998	1016	1033	3	6	9	12	15
6	0.1051	1069	1086	1104	1122	1139	1157	1175	1192	1210	3	6	9	12	15
7	0.1228	1246	1263	1281	1299	1317	1334	1352	1370	1388	3	6	9	12	15
8	0.1405	1423	1441	1459	1477	1495	1512	1530	1548	1566	3	6	9	12	15
9	0.1584	1602	1620	1638	1655	1673	1691	1709	1727	1745	3	6	9	12	15
10	0.1763	1781	1799	1817	1835	1853	1871	1890	1908	1926	3	6	9	12	15
11	0.1944	1962	1980	1998	2016	2035	2053	2071	2089	2107	3	6	9	12	15
12	0.2126	2144	2162	2180	2199	2217	2235	2254	2272	2290	3	6	9	12	15
13	0.2309	2327	2345	2364	2382	2401	2419	2438	2456	2475	3	6	9	12	15
14	0.2493	2512	2530	2549	2568	2586	2605	2623	2642	2661	3	6	9	13	16
15	0.2679	2698	2717	2736	2754	2773	2792	2811	2830	2849	3	6	9	13	16
16	0.2867	2886	2905	2924	2943	2962	2981	3000	3019	3038	3	6	9	13	16
17	0.3057	3076	3096	3115	3134	3153	3172	3191	3211	3230	3	6	10	13	16
18	0.3249	3269	3288	3307	3327	3346	3365	3385	3404	3424	3	6	10	13	16
19	0.3443	3463	3482	3502	3522	3541	3561	3581	3600	3620	3	7	10	13	17
20	0.3640	3659	3679	3699	3719	3739	3759	3779	3799	3819	3	7	10	13	17
21	0.3839	3859	3879	3899	3919	3939	3959	3979	4000	4020	3	7	10	13	17
22	0.4040	4061	4081	4101	4122	4142	4163	4183	4204	4224	3	7	10	13	17
23	0.4245	4265	4286	4307	4327	4348	4369	4390	4411	4431	3	7	10	14	17
24	0.4452	4473	4494	4515	4536	4557	4578	4599	4621	4642	4	7	11	14	18
25	0.4663	4684	4706	4727	4748	4770	4791	4813	4834	4856	4	7	11	14	18
26	0.4877	4899	4921	4942	4964	4986	5008	5029	5051	5073	4	7	11	15	18
27	0.5095	5117	5139	5161	5184	5206	5228	5250	5272	5295	4	7	11	15	18
28	0.5317	5340	5362	5384	5407	5430	5452	5475	5498	5520	4	8	11	15	19
29	0.5543	5566	5589	5612	5635	5658	5681	5704	5727	5750	4	8	12	15	19
30	0.5774	5797	5820	5844	5867	5890	5914	5938	5961	5985	4	8	12	16	20
31	0.6009	6032	6056	6080	6104	6128	6152	6176	6200	6224	4	8	12	16	20
32	0.6249	6273	6297	6322	6346	6371	6395	6420	6445	6469	4	8	12	17	21
33	0.6494	6519	6544	6569	6594	6619	6644	6669	6694	6720	4	8	13	17	21
34	0.6745	6771	6796	6822	6847	6873	6899	6924	6950	6976	4	9	13	17	22
35	0.7002	7028	7054	7080	7107	7133	7159	7186	7212	7239	4	9	13	17	22
36	0.7265	7292	7319	7346	7373	7400	7427	7454	7481	7508	5	9	14	18	23
37	0.7536	7563	7590	7618	7646	7673	7701	7729	7757	7785	5	9	14	19	23
38	0.7813	7841	7869	7898	7926	7954	7983	8012	8040	8069	5	9	14	19	23
39	0.8098	8127	8156	8185	8214	8243	8273	8302	8332	8361	5	10	15	19	24
40	0.8391	8421	8451	8481	8511	8541	8571	8601	8632	8662	5	10	15	20	25
41	0.8693	8724	8754	8785	8816	8847	8878	8910	8941	8972	5	10	16	21	26
42	0.9004	9036	9067	9099	9131	9163	9195	9228	9260	9293	5	11	16	21	27
43	0.9325	9358	9391	9424	9457	9490	9523	9556	9590	9623	6	11	17	22	28
44	0.9657	9691	9725	9759	9793	9827	9861	9896	9930	9965	6	11	17	23	28
45	1.0000	0035	0070	0105	0141	0176	0212	0247	0283	0319	6	12	18	24	30
46	1.0355	0392	0428	0464	0501	0538	0575	0612	0649	0686	6	12	18	25	31
47	1.0724	0761	0799	0837	0875	0913	0951	0990	1028	1067	6	13	19	25	32
48	1.1106	1145	1184	1224	1263	1303	1343	1383	1423	1463	7	13	20	27	33
49	1.1504	1544	1585	1626	1667	1708	1750	1792	1833	1875	7	14	21	27	34
50	1.1918	1960	2002	2045	2088	2131	2174	2218	2261	2305	7	14	22	29	36
51	1.2349	2393	2437	2482	2527	2572	2617	2662	2708	2753	7	15	22	30	37
52	1.2799	2846	2892	2938	2985	3032	3079	3127	3175	3222	8	16	24	31	39
53	1.3270	3319	3367	3416	3465						8	16	24	33	41
						3514	3564	3613	3663	3713	8	17	25	33	42

For 4 significant figures (for small angles) use table ‡, p. 15, to calculate lg tan x°.

TANGENTS tan x°

x°	0' 0°.0	6' 0°.1	12' 0°.2	18' 0°.3	24' 0°.4	30' 0°.5	36' 0°.6	42' 0°.7	48' 0°.8	54' 0°.9	1'	2'	3'	4'	5' ADD
54	1.376	1.381	1.387	1.392	1.397	1.402	1.407	1.412	1.418	1.423	1	2	3	3	4
55	1.428	1.433	1.439	1.444	1.450	1.455	1.460	1.466	1.471	1.477	1	2	3	4	5
56	1.483	1.488	1.494	1.499	1.505	1.511	1.517	1.522	1.528	1.534	1	2	3	4	5
57	1.540	1.546	1.552	1.558	1.564	1.570	1.576	1.582	1.588	1.594	1	2	3	4	5
58	1.600	1.607	1.613	1.619	1.625	1.632	1.638	1.645	1.651	1.658	1	2	3	4	5
59	1.664	1.671	1.678	1.684	1.691	1.698	1.704	1.711	1.718	1.725	1	2	3	5	6
60	1.732	1.739	1.746	1.753	1.760	1.767	1.775	1.782	1.789	1.797	1	2	4	5	6
61	1.804	1.811	1.819	1.827	1.834	1.842	1.849	1.857	1.865	1.873	1	3	4	5	7
62	1.881	1.889	1.897	1.905	1.913	1.921	1.929	1.937	1.946	1.954	1	3	4	5	7
63	1.963	1.971	1.980	1.988	1.997	2.006	2.014	2.023	2.032	2.041	1	3	4	6	7
64	2.050	2.059	2.069	2.078	2.087	2.097	2.106	2.116	2.125	2.135	2	3	5	7	8
65	2.145	2.154	2.164	2.174	2.184	2.194	2.204	2.215	2.225	2.236	2	3	5	7	8
66	2.246	2.257	2.267	2.278	2.289	2.300	2.311	2.322	2.333	2.344	2	4	6	7	9
67	2.356	2.367	2.379	2.391	2.402	2.414	2.426	2.438	2.450	2.463	2	4	6	8	10
68	2.475	2.488	2.500	2.513	2.526	2.539	2.552	2.565	2.578	2.592	2	4	7	9	11
69	2.605	2.619	2.633	2.646	2.660	2.675	2.689	2.703	2.718	2.733	2	5	7	9	12
70	2.747	2.762	2.778	2.793	2.808	2.824	2.840	2.856	2.872	2.888					
71	2.904	2.921	2.937	2.954	2.971	2.989	3.006	3.024	3.042	3.060					
72	3.078	3.096	3.115	3.133	3.152	3.172	3.191	3.211	3.230	3.251					
73	3.271	3.291	3.312	3.333	3.354	3.376	3.398	3.420	3.442	3.465					
74	3.487	3.511	3.534	3.558	3.582	3.606	3.630	3.655	3.681	3.706					
75	3.732	3.758	3.785	3.812	3.839	3.867	3.895	3.923	3.952	3.981					
76	4.011	4.041	4.071	4.102	4.134	4.165	4.198	4.230	4.264	4.297					
77	4.331	4.366	4.402	4.437	4.474	4.511	4.548	4.586	4.625	4.665					
78	4.705	4.745	4.787	4.829	4.872	4.915	4.959	5.005	5.050	5.097					
79	5.145	5.193	5.242	5.292	5.343	5.396	5.449	5.503	5.558	5.614					
80	5.67	5.73	5.79	5.85	5.91	5.98	6.04	6.11	6.17	6.24	1	2	3	4	5
81	6.31	6.39	6.46	6.54	6.61	6.69	6.77	6.85	6.94	7.03	1	3	4	5	7
82	7.12	7.21	7.30	7.40	7.49	7.60	7.70	7.81	7.92	8.03	2	3	5	7	8
83	8.14	8.26	8.39	8.51	8.64	8.78	8.92	9.06	9.21	9.36	2	4	6	9	11
84	9.51	9.68	9.84	10.02	10.20	10.39	10.58	10.78	10.99	11.20	2	5	7	10	12
											3	6	9	11	14
											3	7	10	13	17
											4	7	11	15	18
85	11.4	11.7	11.9	12.2	12.4	12.7	13.0	13.3	13.6	14.0	1	1	2	2	3
86	14.3	14.7	15.1	15.5	15.9	16.3	16.8	17.3	17.9	18.5	1	2	3	3	4
87	19.1	19.7	20.4	21.2	22.0	22.9	23.9	24.9	26.0	27.3	1	2	4	5	6
											2	3	5	7	8
88	28.6	30.1	31.8	33.7	35.8	38.2	40.9	44.1	47.7	52.1	2	4	7	9	11
89	57.3	63.7	71.6	81.8	95.5	114.6	143.2	191.0	286.5	573.0	Interpolation is unreliable for x° > 89°

ADD differences for the range x° = 70–79 (read in sequence):

3 5 8 11 13
3 6 9 11 14
3 6 9 13 16
3 7 10 13 17
3 7 10 14 17
4 7 11 15 18
4 8 12 16 20
4 9 13 17 22
4 9 13 18 22
5 10 14 19 24
5 10 15 21 26
6 11 17 22 28
6 12 18 24 30
7 13 20 26 33
7 14 21 27 34
7 14 22 29 36
8 15 23 30 38
8 16 24 31 39
8 16 25 33 41
8 17 25 34 42
9 18 27 35 44
9 19 28 37 47

For 4 significant figures (for x° ⩾ 80°) find lg tan x°. See p. 13 and table ‡, p. 15.
  Example: lg tan 86° = −lg tan 4° = −(0.6021 + $\bar{2}$.2426) = 1.1553. So tan 86° = 14.30.

$$\cot x° = \tan (90° - x°) = 1/\tan x°$$

$x°$	0' 0°.0	6' 0°.1	12' 0°.2	18' 0°.3	24' 0°.4	30' 0°.5	36' 0°.6	42' 0°.7	48' 0°.8	54' 0°.9	1'	2'	3'	4'	5' ADD
0°	1.0000	0000	0000	0000	0000	0000	0001	0001	0001	0001					
1	1.0002	0002	0002	0003	0003	0003	0004	0004	0005	0006					
2	1.0006	0007	0007	0008	0009	0010	0010	0011	0012	0013					
3	1.0014	0015	0016	0017	0018	0019	0020	0021	0022	0023					
4	1.0024	0026	0027	0028	0030	0031	0032	0034	0035	0037					
5	1.0038	0040	0041	0043	0045	0046	0048	0050	0051	0053	0	1	1	1	2
6	1.0055	0057	0059	0061	0063	0065	0067	0069	0071	0073	0	1	1	1	2
7	1.0075	0077	0079	0082	0084	0086	0089	0091	0093	0096	0	1	1	1	2
8	1.0098	0101	0103	0106	0108	0111	0114	0116	0119	0122	0	1	1	2	2
9	1.0125	0127	0130	0133	0136	0139	0142	0145	0148	0151	0	1	1	2	2
10	1.0154	0157	0161	0164	0167	0170	0174	0177	0180	0184	1	1	2	2	3
11	1.0187	0191	0194	0198	0201	0205	0209	0212	0216	0220	1	1	2	3	3
12	1.0223	0227	0231	0235	0239	0243	0247	0251	0255	0259	1	1	2	3	3
13	1.0263	0267	0271	0276	0280	0284	0288	0293	0297	0302	1	1	2	3	3
14	1.0306	0311	0315	0320	0324	0329	0334	0338	0343	0348	1	2	2	3	4
15	1.0353	0358	0363	0367	0372	0377	0382	0388	0393	0398	1	2	3	3	4
16	1.0403	0408	0413	0419	0424	0429	0435	0440	0446	0451	1	2	3	3	4
17	1.0457	0463	0468	0474	0480	0485	0491	0497	0503	0509	1	2	3	4	5
18	1.0515	0521	0527	0533	0539	0545	0551	0557	0564	0570	1	2	3	4	5
19	1.0576	0583	0589	0595	0602	0608	0615	0622	0628	0635	1	2	3	5	6
20	1.0642	0649	0655	0662	0669	0676	0683	0690	0697	0704	1	2	3	5	6
21	1.0711	0719	0726	0733	0740	0748	0755	0763	0770	0778	1	2	4	5	6
22	1.0785	0793	0801	0808	0816	0824	0832	0840	0848	0856	1	3	4	5	7
23	1.0864	0872	0880	0888	0896	0904	0913	0921	0929	0938	1	3	4	5	7
24	1.0946	0955	0963	0972	0981	0989	0998	1007	1016	1025	1	3	4	6	7
25	1.1034	1043	1052	1061	1070	1079	1089	1098	1107	1117	2	3	5	6	8
26	1.1126	1136	1145	1155	1164	1174	1184	1194	1203	1213	2	3	5	7	8
27	1.1223	1233	1243	1253	1264	1274	1284	1294	1305	1315	2	3	5	7	8
28	1.1326	1336	1347	1357	1368	1379	1390	1401	1412	1423	2	4	5	7	9
29	1.1434	1445	1456	1467	1478	1490	1501	1512	1524	1535	2	4	6	7	9
30	1.1547	1559	1570	1582	1594	1606	1618	1630	1642	1654	2	4	6	8	10
31	1.1666	1679	1691	1703	1716	1728	1741	1753	1766	1779	2	4	6	9	11
32	1.1792	1805	1818	1831	1844	1857	1870	1883	1897	1910	2	4	7	9	11
33	1.1924	1937	1951	1964	1978	1992	2006	2020	2034	2048	2	5	7	9	12
34	1.2062	2076	2091	2105	2120	2134	2149	2163	2178	2193	2	5	7	10	12
35	1.2208	2223	2238	2253	2268	2283	2299	2314	2329	2345	3	5	8	10	13
36	1.2361	2376	2392	2408	2424	2440	2456	2472	2489	2505	3	5	8	11	13
37	1.2521	2538	2554	2571	2588	2605	2622	2639	2656	2673	3	6	8	11	14
38	1.2690	2708	2725	2742	2760	2778	2796	2813	2831	2849	3	6	9	12	15
39	1.2868	2886	2904	2923	2941	2960	2978	2997	3016	3035	3	6	9	13	16
40	1.3054	3073	3093	3112	3131	3151	3171	3190	3210	3230	3	7	10	13	17
41	1.3250	3270	3291	3311	3331	3352	3373	3393	3414	3435	3	7	10	14	17
42	1.3456	3478	3499	3520	3542	3563	3585	3607	3629	3651	4	7	11	15	18
43	1.3673	3696	3718	3741	3763	3786	3809	3832	3855	3878	4	8	11	15	19
44	1.3902	3925	3949	3972	3996	4020	4044	4069	4093	4118	4	8	12	16	20
45	1.4142	4167	4192	4217	4242	4267	4293	4318	4344	4370	4	8	13	17	21
46	1.4396	4422	4448	4474	4501	4527	4554	4581	4608	4635	4	9	13	18	22
47	1.4663	4690	4718	4746	4774	4802	4830	4859	4887	4916	5	9	14	19	23
48	1.4945	4974	5003	5032	5062	5092	5121	5151	5182	5212	5	10	15	20	25
49	1.5243	5273	5304	5335	5366	5398	5429	5461	5493	5525	5	10	16	21	26
50	1.5557	5590	5622	5655	5688	5721	5755	5788	5822	5856	6	11	17	22	28
51	1.5890	5925	5959	5994	6029	6064	6099	6135	6171	6207	6	12	18	23	29
52	1.6243	6279	6316	6353	6390	6427	6464	6502	6540	6578	6	12	19	25	31
53	1.6616	6655	6694	6733	6772	6812	6852	6892	6932	6972	7	13	20	27	33
54	1.7013	7054	7095	7137	7179	7221	7263	7305	7348	7391	7	14	21	28	35

$$\mathbf{cosec}\ x° = \mathbf{sec}\ (90° - x°)$$

SECANTS $\sec x°$

$x°$	0' 0°.0	6' 0°.1	12' 0°.2	18' 0°.3	24' 0°.4	30' 0°.5	36' 0°.6	42' 0°.7	48' 0°.8	54' 0°.9
55°	1.743	1.748	1.752	1.757	1.761	1.766	1.770	1.775	1.779	1.784
56	1.788	1.793	1.798	1.802	1.807	1.812	1.817	1.821	1.826	1.831
57	1.836	1.841	1.846	1.851	1.856	1.861	1.866	1.871	1.877	1.882
58	1.887	1.892	1.898	1.903	1.908	1.914	1.919	1.925	1.930	1.936
59	1.942	1.947	1.953	1.959	1.964	1.970	1.976	1.982	1.988	1.994
60	2.000	2.006	2.012	2.018	2.025	2.031	2.037	2.043	2.050	2.056
61	2.063	2.069	2.076	2.082	2.089	2.096	2.103	2.109	2.116	2.123
62	2.130	2.137	2.144	2.151	2.158	2.166	2.173	2.180	2.188	2.195
63	2.203	2.210	2.218	2.226	2.233	2.241	2.249	2.257	2.265	2.273
64	2.281	2.289	2.298	2.306	2.314	2.323	2.331	2.340	2.349	2.357
65	2.366	2.375	2.384	2.393	2.402	2.411	2.421	2.430	2.439	2.449
66	2.459	2.468	2.478	2.488	2.498	2.508	2.518	2.528	2.538	2.549
67	2.559	2.570	2.581	2.591	2.602	2.613	2.624	2.635	2.647	2.658
68	2.669	2.681	2.693	2.705	2.716	2.729	2.741	2.753	2.765	2.778
69	2.790	2.803	2.816	2.829	2.842	2.855	2.869	2.882	2.896	2.910
70	2.924	2.938	2.952	2.967	2.981	2.996	3.011	3.026	3.041	3.056
71	3.072	3.087	3.103	3.119	3.135	3.152	3.168	3.185	3.202	3.219
72	3.236	3.254	3.271	3.289	3.307	3.326	3.344	3.363	3.382	3.401
73	3.420	3.440	3.460	3.480	3.500	3.521	3.542	3.563	3.584	3.606
74	3.628	3.650	3.673	3.695	3.719	3.742	3.766	3.790	3.814	3.839
75	3.864	3.889	3.915	3.941	3.967	3.994	4.021	4.049	4.077	4.105
76	4.134	4.163	4.192	4.222	4.253	4.284	4.315	4.347	4.379	4.412
77	4.445	4.479	4.514	4.549	4.584	4.620	4.657	4.694	4.732	4.771
78	4.810	4.850	4.890	4.931	4.973	5.016	5.059	5.103	5.148	5.194
79	5.241	5.288	5.337	5.386	5.436	5.487	5.540	5.593	5.647	5.702
80	5.76	5.82	5.88	5.94	6.00	6.06	6.12	6.19	6.25	6.32
81	6.39	6.46	6.54	6.61	6.69	6.77	6.85	6.93	7.01	7.10
82	7.19	7.28	7.37	7.46	7.56	7.66	7.76	7.87	7.98	8.09
83	8.21	8.32	8.45	8.57	8.70	8.83	8.97	9.11	9.26	9.41
84	9.57	9.73	9.90	10.07	10.25	10.43	10.63	10.83	11.03	11.25
85	11.5	11.7	12.0	12.2	12.5	12.7	13.0	13.3	13.7	14.0
86	14.3	14.7	15.1	15.5	15.9	16.4	16.9	17.4	17.9	18.5
87	19.1	19.8	20.5	21.2	22.0	22.9	23.9	24.9	26.0	27.3
88	28.7	30.2	31.8	33.7	35.8	38.2	40.9	44.1	47.7	52.1
89	57.3	63.7	71.6	81.9	95.5	114.6	143.2	191.0	286.5	573.0

ADD

1'	2'	3'	4'	5'
1	1	2	3	3
1	2	2	3	4
1	2	3	3	4
1	2	3	4	5
1	2	3	4	5
1	2	3	4	5
1	2	3	5	6
1	2	4	5	6
1	3	4	5	7
1	3	4	5	7
2	3	5	6	8
2	3	5	7	8
2	4	6	7	9
2	4	6	8	10
2	4	7	9	11
2	5	7	10	12
3	5	8	11	13
3	6	9	12	15
3	7	10	14	17
4	8	11	15	19
4	8	12	16	20
4	9	13	17	22
5	9	14	19	23
5	10	15	20	25
5	11	16	21	27
6	12	18	23	29
6	13	19	25	32
7	14	20	27	34
7	14	22	29	36
8	15	23	31	38
8	16	24	32	40
8	17	25	33	42
9	18	27	35	44
9	19	28	37	47
1	2	3	4	5
1	3	4	5	7
2	3	5	6	8
2	4	6	7	9
2	4	6	8	10
2	5	7	10	12
3	6	9	11	14
3	7	10	14	17
1	1	2	2	3
1	2	3	3	4
1	3	4	5	7
2	3	5	7	8
2	4	7	9	11

Interpolation
is unreliable
for $x° > 89°$

For 4 significant figures (for $x° \geqslant 80°$) find $\lg \sec x° = -\lg \cos x°$. See p. 11.

SQUARES x^2

x	0	1	2	3	4	5	6	7	8	9	1	2	3	4	5	6	7	8	9
														ADD					
1.0	1.000	1.020	1.040	1.061	1.082	1.103	1.124	1.145	1.166	1.188	2	4	6	8	10	13	15	17	19
1.1	1.210	1.232	1.254	1.277	1.300	1.323	1.346	1.369	1.392	1.416	2	5	7	9	11	14	16	18	21
1.2	1.440	1.464	1.488	1.513	1.538	1.563	1.588	1.613	1.638	1.664	2	5	7	10	12	15	17	20	22
1.3	1.690	1.716	1.742	1.769	1.796	1.823	1.850	1.877	1.904	1.932	3	5	8	11	13	16	19	22	24
1.4	1.960	1.988	2.016	2.045	2.074	2.103	2.132	2.161	2.190	2.220	3	6	9	12	14	17	20	23	26
1.5	2.250	2.280	2.310	2.341	2.372	2.403	2.434	2.465	2.496	2.528	3	6	9	12	15	19	22	25	28
1.6	2.560	2.592	2.624	2.657	2.690	2.723	2.756	2.789	2.822	2.856	3	7	10	13	16	20	23	26	30
1.7	2.890	2.924	2.958	2.993	3.028	3.063	3.098	3.133	3.168	3.204	3	7	10	14	17	21	24	28	31
1.8	3.240	3.276	3.312	3.349	3.386	3.423	3.460	3.497	3.534	3.572	4	7	11	15	18	22	26	30	33
1.9	3.610	3.648	3.686	3.725	3.764	3.803	3.842	3.881	3.920	3.960	4	8	12	16	19	23	27	31	35
2.0	4.000	4.040	4.080	4.121	4.162	4.203	4.244	4.285	4.326	4.368	4	8	12	16	20	25	29	33	37
2.1	4.410	4.452	4.494	4.537	4.580	4.623	4.666	4.709	4.752	4.796	4	9	13	17	21	26	30	34	39
2.2	4.840	4.884	4.928	4.973	5.018	5.063	5.108	5.153	5.198	5.244	4	9	13	18	22	27	31	36	40
2.3	5.290	5.336	5.382	5.429	5.476	5.523	5.570	5.617	5.664	5.712	5	9	14	19	23	28	33	38	42
2.4	5.760	5.808	5.856	5.905	5.954	6.003	6.052	6.101	6.150	6.200	5	10	15	20	24	29	34	39	44
2.5	6.250	6.300	6.350	6.401	6.452	6.503	6.554	6.605	6.656	6.708	5	10	15	20	25	31	36	41	46
2.6	6.760	6.812	6.864	6.917	6.970	7.023	7.076	7.129	7.182	7.236	5	11	16	21	26	32	37	42	48
2.7	7.290	7.344	7.398	7.453	7.508	7.563	7.618	7.673	7.728	7.784	5	11	16	22	27	33	38	44	49
2.8	7.840	7.896	7.952	8.009	8.066	8.123	8.180	8.237	8.294	8.352	6	11	17	23	28	34	40	46	51
2.9	8.410	8.468	8.526	8.585	8.644	8.703	8.762	8.821	8.880	8.940	6	12	18	24	29	35	41	47	53
3.0	9.000	9.060	9.120	9.181	9.242	9.303	9.364	9.425	9.486	9.548	6	12	18	24	30	37	43	49	55
3.1	9.610	9.672	9.734	9.797	9.860	9.923	9.986				6	13	19	25	31	38	44	50	57
								10.05	10.11	10.18	1	1	2	2	3	4	4	5	5
3.2	10.24	10.30	10.37	10.43	10.50	10.56	10.63	10.69	10.76	10.82	1	1	2	2	3	4	4	5	5
3.3	10.89	10.96	11.02	11.09	11.16	11.22	11.29	11.36	11.42	11.49	1	1	2	3	3	4	5	6	6
3.4	11.56	11.63	11.70	11.76	11.83	11.90	11.97	12.04	12.11	12.18	1	1	2	3	3	4	5	6	6
3.5	12.25	12.32	12.39	12.46	12.53	12.60	12.67	12.74	12.82	12.89	1	1	2	3	4	4	5	6	6
3.6	12.96	13.03	13.10	13.18	13.25	13.32	13.40	13.47	13.54	13.62	1	1	2	3	4	4	5	6	6
3.7	13.69	13.76	13.84	13.91	13.99	14.06	14.14	14.21	14.29	14.36	1	2	2	3	4	5	6	6	7
3.8	14.44	14.52	14.59	14.67	14.75	14.82	14.90	14.98	15.05	15.13	1	2	2	3	4	5	6	6	7
3.9	15.21	15.29	15.37	15.44	15.52	15.60	15.68	15.76	15.84	15.92	1	2	2	3	4	5	6	6	7
4.0	16.00	16.08	16.16	16.24	16.32	16.40	16.48	16.56	16.65	16.73	1	2	2	3	4	5	6	6	7
4.1	16.81	16.89	16.97	17.06	17.14	17.22	17.31	17.39	17.47	17.56	1	2	2	3	4	5	6	6	7
4.2	17.64	17.72	17.81	17.89	17.98	18.06	18.15	18.23	18.32	18.40	1	2	2	3	4	5	6	6	7
4.3	18.49	18.58	18.66	18.75	18.84	18.92	19.01	19.10	19.18	19.27	1	2	3	4	4	5	6	7	8
4.4	19.36	19.45	19.54	19.62	19.71	19.80	19.89	19.98	20.07	20.16	1	2	3	4	4	5	6	7	8
4.5	20.25	20.34	20.43	20.52	20.61	20.70	20.79	20.88	20.98	21.07	1	2	3	4	5	5	6	7	8
4.6	21.16	21.25	21.34	21.44	21.53	21.62	21.72	21.81	21.90	22.00	1	2	3	4	5	5	6	7	8
4.7	22.09	22.18	22.28	22.37	22.47	22.56	22.66	22.75	22.85	22.94	1	2	3	4	5	6	7	8	9
4.8	23.04	23.14	23.23	23.33	23.43	23.52	23.62	23.72	23.81	23.91	1	2	3	4	5	6	7	8	9
4.9	24.01	24.11	24.21	24.30	24.40	24.50	24.60	24.70	24.80	24.90	1	2	3	4	5	6	7	8	9
5.0	25.00	25.10	25.20	25.30	25.40	25.50	25.60	25.70	25.81	25.91	1	2	3	4	5	6	7	8	9
5.1	26.01	26.11	26.21	26.32	26.42	26.52	26.63	26.73	26.83	26.94	1	2	3	4	5	6	7	8	9
5.2	27.04	27.14	27.25	27.35	27.46	27.56	27.67	27.77	27.88	27.98	1	2	3	4	5	6	7	8	9
5.3	28.09	28.20	28.30	28.41	28.52	28.62	28.73	28.84	28.94	29.05	1	2	3	4	5	7	8	9	10
5.4	29.16	29.27	29.38	29.48	29.59	29.70	29.81	29.92	30.03	30.14	1	2	3	4	5	7	8	9	10
5.5	30.25	30.36	30.47	30.58	30.69	30.80	30.91	31.02	31.14	31.25	1	2	3	4	6	7	8	9	10
5.6	31.36	31.47	31.58	31.70	31.81	31.92	32.04	32.15	32.26	32.38	1	2	3	4	6	7	8	9	10
5.7	32.49	32.60	32.72	32.83	32.95	33.06	33.18	33.29	33.41	33.52	1	2	4	5	6	7	8	10	11
5.8	33.64	33.76	33.87	33.99	34.11	34.22	34.34	34.46	34.57	34.69	1	2	4	5	6	7	8	10	11
5.9	34.81	34.93	35.05	35.16	35.28	35.40	35.52	35.64	35.76	35.88	1	2	4	5	6	7	8	10	11

x	0	1	2	3	4	5	6	7	8	9	1	2	3	4	5	6	7	8	9
														ADD					
6.0	36.00	36.12	36.24	36.36	36.48	36.60	36.72	36.84	36.97	37.09	1	2	4	5	6	7	8	10	11
6.1	37.21	37.33	37.45	37.58	37.70	37.82	37.95	38.07	38.19	38.32	1	2	4	5	6	7	8	10	11
6.2	38.44	38.56	38.69	38.81	38.94	39.06	39.19	39.31	39.44	39.56	1	2	4	5	6	7	8	10	11
6.3	39.69	39.82	39.94	40.07	40.20	40.32	40.45	40.58	40.70	40.83	1	3	4	5	6	8	9	10	12
6.4	40.96	41.09	41.22	41.34	41.47	41.60	41.73	41.86	41.99	42.12	1	3	4	5	6	8	9	10	12
6.5	42.25	42.38	42.51	42.64	42.77	42.90	43.03	43.16	43.30	43.43	1	3	4	5	7	8	9	10	12
6.6	43.56	43.69	43.82	43.96	44.09	44.22	44.36	44.49	44.62	44.76	1	3	4	5	7	8	9	10	12
6.7	44.89	45.02	45.16	45.29	45.43	45.56	45.70	45.83	45.97	46.10	1	3	4	6	7	8	10	11	13
6.8	46.24	46.38	46.51	46.65	46.79	46.92	47.06	47.20	47.33	47.47	1	3	4	6	7	8	10	11	13
6.9	47.61	47.75	47.89	48.02	48.16	48.30	48.44	48.58	48.72	48.86	1	3	4	6	7	8	10	11	13
7.0	49.00	49.14	49.28	49.42	49.56	49.70	49.84	49.98	50.13	50.27	1	3	4	6	7	8	10	11	13
7.1	50.41	50.55	50.69	50.84	50.98	51.12	51.27	51.41	51.55	51.70	1	3	4	6	7	8	10	11	13
7.2	51.84	51.98	52.13	52.27	52.42	52.56	52.71	52.85	53.00	53.14	1	3	4	6	7	8	10	11	13
7.3	53.29	53.44	53.58	53.73	53.88	54.02	54.17	54.32	54.46	54.61	1	3	4	6	7	9	10	12	13
7.4	54.76	54.91	55.06	55.20	55.35	55.50	55.65	55.80	55.95	56.10	1	3	4	6	7	9	10	12	13
7.5	56.25	56.40	56.55	56.70	56.85	57.00	57.15	57.30	57.46	57.61	2	3	5	6	8	9	11	12	14
7.6	57.76	57.91	58.06	58.22	58.37	58.52	58.68	58.83	58.98	59.14	2	3	5	6	8	9	11	12	14
7.7	59.29	59.44	59.60	59.75	59.91	60.06	60.22	60.37	60.53	60.68	2	3	5	6	8	10	11	13	14
7.8	60.84	61.00	61.15	61.31	61.47	61.62	61.78	61.94	62.09	62.25	2	3	5	6	8	10	11	13	14
7.9	62.41	62.57	62.73	62.88	63.04	63.20	63.36	63.52	63.68	63.84	2	3	5	6	8	10	11	13	14
8.0	64.00	64.16	64.32	64.48	64.64	64.80	64.96	65.12	65.29	65.45	2	3	5	6	8	10	11	13	14
8.1	65.61	65.77	65.93	66.10	66.26	66.42	66.59	66.75	66.91	67.08	2	3	5	6	8	10	11	13	14
8.2	67.24	67.40	67.57	67.73	67.90	68.06	68.23	68.39	68.56	68.72	2	3	5	6	8	10	11	13	14
8.3	68.89	69.06	69.22	69.39	69.56	69.72	69.89	70.06	70.22	70.39	2	3	5	7	8	10	12	14	15
8.4	70.56	70.73	70.90	71.06	71.23	71.40	71.57	71.74	71.91	72.08	2	3	5	7	8	10	12	14	15
8.5	72.25	72.42	72.59	72.76	72.93	73.10	73.27	73.44	73.62	73.79	2	3	5	7	9	10	12	14	15
8.6	73.96	74.13	74.30	74.48	74.65	74.82	75.00	75.17	75.34	75.52	2	3	5	7	9	10	12	14	15
8.7	75.69	75.86	76.04	76.21	76.39	76.56	76.74	76.91	77.09	77.26	2	4	5	7	9	11	13	14	16
8.8	77.44	77.62	77.79	77.97	78.15	78.32	78.50	78.68	78.85	79.03	2	4	5	7	9	11	13	14	16
8.9	79.21	79.39	79.57	79.74	79.92	80.10	80.28	80.46	80.64	80.82	2	4	5	7	9	11	13	14	16
9.0	81.00	81.18	81.36	81.54	81.72	81.90	82.08	82.26	82.45	82.63	2	4	5	7	9	11	13	14	16
9.1	82.81	82.99	83.17	83.36	83.54	83.72	83.91	84.09	84.27	84.46	2	4	5	7	9	11	13	14	16
9.2	84.64	84.82	85.01	85.19	85.38	85.56	85.75	85.93	86.12	86.30	2	4	5	7	9	11	13	14	16
9.3	86.49	86.68	86.86	87.05	87.24	87.42	87.61	87.80	87.98	88.17	2	4	6	8	9	11	13	15	17
9.4	88.36	88.55	88.74	88.92	89.11	89.30	89.49	89.68	89.87	90.06	2	4	6	8	9	11	13	15	17
9.5	90.25	90.44	90.63	90.82	91.01	91.20	91.39	91.58	91.78	91.97	2	4	6	8	10	11	13	15	17
9.6	92.16	92.35	92.54	92.74	92.93	93.12	93.32	93.51	93.70	93.90	2	4	6	8	10	11	13	15	17
9.7	94.09	94.28	94.48	94.67	94.87	95.06	95.26	95.45	95.65	95.84	2	4	6	8	10	12	14	16	18
9.8	96.04	96.24	96.43	96.63	96.83	97.02	97.22	97.42	97.61	97.81	2	4	6	8	10	12	14	16	18
9.9	98.01	98.21	98.41	98.60	98.80	99.00	99.20	99.40	99.60	99.80	2	4	6	8	10	12	14	16	18

Examples:

$$(1.43)^2 = 2.045 \qquad (6.935)^2 = 48.09$$
$$(232.8)^2 = (2.328 \times 10^2)^2 = 5.420 \times 10^4$$
$$(0.007035)^2 = (7.035 \times 10^{-3})^2 = 49.49 \times 10^{-6} = 0.00004949$$

It is sometimes more accurate to use:

$$x^2 = 4 \times (\tfrac{1}{2}x)^2 \quad \text{or} \quad x^2 = \tfrac{1}{4} \times (2x)^2$$

Thus:

$$(3.26)^2 = 4 \times (1.63)^2 = 4 \times 2.657 = 10.628$$

with an error of at most 2 in the last decimal place.

SQUARE ROOTS $\quad \sqrt{x}$ or $x^{\frac{1}{2}}$

x	0	1	2	3	4	5	6	7	8	9	1 2 3	4 5 6	7 8 9
												ADD	
1.0	1.000	1.005	1.010	1.015	1.020	1.025	1.030	1.034	1.039	1.044	0 1 1	2 2 3	3 4 4
1.1	1.049	1.054	1.058	1.063	1.068	1.072	1.077	1.082	1.086	1.091	0 1 1	2 2 3	3 4 4
1.2	1.095	1.100	1.105	1.109	1.114	1.118	1.122	1.127	1.131	1.136	0 1 1	2 2 2	3 3 4
1.3	1.140	1.145	1.149	1.153	1.158	1.162	1.166	1.170	1.175	1.179	0 1 1	2 2 2	3 3 4
1.4	1.183	1.187	1.192	1.196	1.200	1.204	1.208	1.212	1.217	1.221	0 1 1	2 2 2	3 3 4
1.5	1.225	1.229	1.233	1.237	1.241	1.245	1.249	1.253	1.257	1.261	0 1 1	2 2 2	3 3 4
1.6	1.265	1.269	1.273	1.277	1.281	1.285	1.288	1.292	1.296	1.300	0 1 1	2 2 2	3 3 4
1.7	1.304	1.308	1.311	1.315	1.319	1.323	1.327	1.330	1.334	1.338	0 1 1	2 2 2	3 3 4
1.8	1.342	1.345	1.349	1.353	1.356	1.360	1.364	1.367	1.371	1.375	0 1 1	2 2 2	3 3 4
1.9	1.378	1.382	1.386	1.389	1.393	1.396	1.400	1.404	1.407	1.411	0 1 1	2 2 2	3 3 4
2.	1.414	1.449	1.483								3 7 10	14 17 20	24 27 31
				1.517	1.549	1.581	1.612				3 6 9	12 16 19	22 25 28
								1.643	1.673	1.703	3 6 9	12 15 17	20 23 26
3.	1.732	1.761	1.789	1.817	1.844						3 6 8	11 14 17	20 22 25
						1.871	1.897	1.924	1.949	1.975	3 5 8	10 13 16	18 21 2.
4.	2.000	2.025	2.049	2.074	2.098						2 5 7	10 12 14	17 19 22
						2.121	2.145	2.168	2.191	2.214	2 5 7	9 12 14	16 18 21
5.	2.236	2.258	2.280	2.302	2.324	2.345	2.366	2.387	2.408	2.429	2 4 6	8 11 13	15 17 19
6.	2.449	2.470	2.490	2.510	2.530	2.550	2.569	2.588	2.608	2.627	2 4 6	8 10 12	14 16 18
7.	2.646	2.665	2.683	2.702	2.720	2.739	2.757	2.775	2.793	2.811	2 4 5	7 9 11	13 14 16
8.	2.828	2.846	2.864	2.881	2.898	2.915	2.933	2.950	2.966	2.983	2 3 5	7 9 10	12 14 15
9.	3.000	3.017	3.033	3.050	3.066	3.082	3.098	3.114	3.130	3.146	2 3 5	6 8 10	11 13 14
10.	3.162	3.178	3.194	3.209	3.225	3.240	3.256	3.271	3.286	3.302	2 3 5	6 8 9	11 12 14
11.	3.317	3.332	3.347	3.362	3.376	3.391	3.406	3.421	3.435	3.450	1 3 4	6 7 9	10 12 13
12.	3.464	3.479	3.493	3.507	3.521	3.536	3.550	3.564	3.578	3.592	1 3 4	6 7 8	10 11 13
13.	3.606	3.619	3.633	3.647	3.661	3.674	3.688	3.701	3.715	3.728	1 3 4	6 7 8	10 11 12
14.	3.742	3.755	3.768	3.782	3.795	3.808	3.821	3.834	3.847	3.860	1 3 4	5 7 8	9 10 12
15.	3.873	3.886	3.899	3.912	3.924	3.937	3.950	3.962	3.975	3.987	1 3 4	5 6 8	9 10 12
16.	4.000	4.012	4.025	4.037	4.050	4.062	4.074	4.087	4.099	4.111	1 2 4	5 6 7	8 10 11
17.	4.123	4.135	4.147	4.159	4.171	4.183	4.195	4.207	4.219	4.231	1 2 4	5 6 7	8 10 11
18.	4.243	4.254	4.266	4.278	4.290	4.301	4.313	4.324	4.336	4.347	1 2 4	5 6 7	8 10 11
19.	4.359	4.370	4.382	4.393	4.405	4.416	4.427	4.438	4.450	4.461	1 2 3	4 6 7	8 9 10
20.	4.472	4.483	4.494	4.506	4.517	4.528	4.539	4.550	4.561	4.572	1 2 3	4 6 7	8 9 10
21.	4.583	4.593	4.604	4.615	4.626	4.637	4.648	4.658	4.669	4.680	1 2 3	4 5 7	8 9 10
22.	4.690	4.701	4.712	4.722	4.733	4.743	4.754	4.764	4.775	4.785	1 2 3	4 5 7	8 9 10
23.	4.796	4.806	4.817	4.827	4.837	4.848	4.858	4.868	4.879	4.889	1 2 3	4 5 6	7 8 9
24.	4.899	4.909	4.919	4.930	4.940	4.950	4.960	4.970	4.980	4.990	1 2 3	4 5 6	7 8 9
25.	5.000	5.010	5.020	5.030	5.040	5.050	5.060	5.070	5.079	5.089	1 2 3	4 5 6	7 8 9
26.	5.099	5.109	5.119	5.128	5.138	5.148	5.158	5.167	5.177	5.187	1 2 3	4 5 6	7 8 9
27.	5.196	5.206	5.215	5.225	5.235	5.244	5.254	5.263	5.273	5.282	1 2 3	4 5 6	7 8 9
28.	5.292	5.301	5.310	5.320	5.329	5.339	5.348	5.357	5.367	5.376	1 2 3	4 5 5	6 7 8
29.	5.385	5.394	5.404	5.413	5.422	5.431	5.441	5.450	5.459	5.468	1 2 3	4 5 5	6 7 8
30.	5.477	5.486	5.495	5.505	5.514	5.523	5.532	5.541	5.550	5.559	1 2 3	4 5 5	6 7 8
31.	5.568	5.577	5.586	5.595	5.604	5.612	5.621	5.630	5.639	5.648	1 2 3	4 4 5	6 7 8
32.	5.657	5.666	5.675	5.683	5.692	5.701	5.710	5.718	5.727	5.736	1 2 3	4 4 5	6 7 8
33.	5.745	5.753	5.762	5.771	5.779	5.788	5.797	5.805	5.814	5.822	1 2 3	4 4 5	6 7 8
34.	5.831	5.840	5.848	5.857	5.865	5.874	5.882	5.891	5.899	5.908	1 2 3	4 4 5	6 7 8
35.	5.916	5.925	5.933	5.941	5.950	5.958	5.967	5.975	5.983	5.992	1 2 2	3 4 5	6 6 7
36.	6.000	6.008	6.017	6.025	6.033	6.042	6.050	6.058	6.066	6.075	1 2 2	3 4 5	6 6 7
37.	6.083	6.091	6.099	6.107	6.116	6.124	6.132	6.140	6.148	6.156	1 2 2	3 4 5	6 6 7
38.	6.164	6.173	6.181	6.189	6.197	6.205	6.213	6.221	6.229	6.237	1 2 2	3 4 5	6 6 7
39.	6.245	6.253	6.261	6.269	6.277	6.285	6.293	6.301	6.309	6.317	1 2 2	3 4 5	6 6 7
40.	6.325	6.332	6.340	6.348	6.356	6.364	6.372	6.380	6.387	6.395	1 2 2	3 4 5	6 6 7
41.	6.403	6.411	6.419	6.427	6.434	6.442	6.450	6.458	6.465	6.473	1 2 2	3 4 5	6 6 7
42.	6.481	6.488	6.496	6.504	6.512	6.519	6.527	6.535	6.542	6.550	1 2 2	3 4 5	6 6 7
43.	6.557	6.565	6.573	6.580	6.588	6.595	6.603	6.611	6.618	6.626	1 2 2	3 4 5	6 6 7
44.	6.633	6.641	6.648	6.656	6.663	6.671	6.678	6.686	6.693	6.701	1 2 2	3 4 5	6 6 7

SQUARE ROOTS $\quad \sqrt{x}$ or $x^{\frac{1}{2}}$

x	0	1	2	3	4	5	6	7	8	9	1	2	3	4	5	6	7	8	9
															ADD				
45.	6.708	6.716	6.723	6.731	6.738	6.745	6.753	6.760	6.768	6.775	1	1	2	3	4	4	5	6	6
46.	6.782	6.790	6.797	6.804	6.812	6.819	6.826	6.834	6.841	6.848	1	1	2	3	4	4	5	6	6
47.	6.856	6.863	6.870	6.877	6.885	6.892	6.899	6.907	6.914	6.921	1	1	2	3	4	4	5	6	6
48.	6.928	6.935	6.943	6.950	6.957	6.964	6.971	6.979	6.986	6.993	1	1	2	3	4	4	5	6	6
49.	7.000	7.007	7.014	7.021	7.029	7.036	7.043	7.050	7.057	7.064	1	1	2	3	4	4	5	6	6
50.	7.071	7.078	7.085	7.092	7.099	7.106	7.113	7.120	7.127	7.134	1	1	2	3	4	4	5	6	6
51.	7.141	7.148	7.155	7.162	7.169	7.176	7.183	7.190	7.197	7.204	1	1	2	3	4	4	5	6	6
52.	7.211	7.218	7.225	7.232	7.239	7.246	7.253	7.259	7.266	7.273	1	1	2	3	3	4	5	6	6
53.	7.280	7.287	7.294	7.301	7.308	7.314	7.321	7.328	7.335	7.342	1	1	2	3	3	4	5	6	6
54.	7.348	7.355	7.362	7.369	7.376	7.382	7.389	7.396	7.403	7.409	1	1	2	3	3	4	5	6	6
55.	7.416	7.423	7.430	7.436	7.443	7.450	7.457	7.463	7.470	7.477	1	1	2	3	3	4	5	6	6
56.	7.483	7.490	7.497	7.503	7.510	7.517	7.523	7.530	7.537	7.543	1	1	2	3	3	4	5	6	6
57.	7.550	7.556	7.563	7.570	7.576	7.583	7.589	7.596	7.603	7.609	1	1	2	3	3	4	5	6	6
58.	7.616	7.622	7.629	7.635	7.642	7.649	7.655	7.662	7.668	7.675	1	1	2	2	3	4	4	5	5
59.	7.681	7.688	7.694	7.701	7.707	7.714	7.720	7.727	7.733	7.740	1	1	2	2	3	4	4	5	5
60.	7.746	7.752	7.759	7.765	7.772	7.778	7.785	7.791	7.797	7.804	1	1	2	2	3	4	4	5	5
61.	7.810	7.817	7.823	7.829	7.836	7.842	7.849	7.855	7.861	7.868	1	1	2	2	3	4	4	5	5
62.	7.874	7.880	7.887	7.893	7.899	7.906	7.912	7.918	7.925	7.931	1	1	2	2	3	4	4	5	5
63.	7.937	7.944	7.950	7.956	7.962	7.969	7.975	7.981	7.987	7.994	1	1	2	2	3	4	4	5	5
64.	8.000	8.006	8.012	8.019	8.025	8.031	8.037	8.044	8.050	8.056	1	1	2	2	3	4	4	5	5
65.	8.062	8.068	8.075	8.081	8.087	8.093	8.099	8.106	8.112	8.118	1	1	2	2	3	4	4	5	5
66.	8.124	8.130	8.136	8.142	8.149	8.155	8.161	8.167	8.173	8.179	1	1	2	2	3	4	4	5	5
67.	8.185	8.191	8.198	8.204	8.210	8.216	8.222	8.228	8.234	8.240	1	1	2	2	3	4	4	5	5
68.	8.246	8.252	8.258	8.264	8.270	8.276	8.283	8.289	8.295	8.301	1	1	2	2	3	4	4	5	5
69.	8.307	8.313	8.319	8.325	8.331	8.337	8.343	8.349	8.355	8.361	1	1	2	2	3	4	4	5	5
70.	8.367	8.373	8.379	8.385	8.390	8.396	8.402	8.408	8.414	8.420	1	1	2	2	3	4	4	5	5
71.	8.426	8.432	8.438	8.444	8.450	8.456	8.462	8.468	8.473	8.479	1	1	2	2	3	4	4	5	5
72.	8.485	8.491	8.497	8.503	8.509	8.515	8.521	8.526	8.532	8.538	1	1	2	2	3	4	4	5	5
73.	8.544	8.550	8.556	8.562	8.567	8.573	8.579	8.585	8.591	8.597	1	1	2	2	3	4	4	5	5
74.	8.602	8.608	8.614	8.620	8.626	8.631	8.637	8.643	8.649	8.654	1	1	2	2	3	4	4	5	5
75.	8.660	8.666	8.672	8.678	8.683	8.689	8.695	8.701	8.706	8.712	1	1	2	2	3	4	4	5	5
76.	8.718	8.724	8.729	8.735	8.741	8.746	8.752	8.758	8.764	8.769	1	1	2	2	3	4	4	5	5
77.	8.775	8.781	8.786	8.792	8.798	8.803	8.809	8.815	8.820	8.826	1	1	2	2	3	4	4	5	5
78.	8.832	8.837	8.843	8.849	8.854	8.860	8.866	8.871	8.877	8.883	1	1	2	2	3	4	4	5	5
79.	8.888	8.894	8.899	8.905	8.911	8.916	8.922	8.927	8.933	8.939	1	1	2	2	3	4	4	5	5
80.	8.944	8.950	8.955	8.961	8.967	8.972	8.978	8.983	8.989	8.994	1	1	2	2	3	4	4	5	5
81.	9.000	9.006	9.011	9.017	9.022	9.028	9.033	9.039	9.044	9.050	1	1	2	2	3	4	4	5	5
82.	9.055	9.061	9.066	9.072	9.077	9.083	9.088	9.094	9.099	9.105	1	1	2	2	3	4	4	5	5
83.	9.110	9.116	9.121	9.127	9.132	9.138	9.143	9.149	9.154	9.160	1	1	2	2	3	3	4	4	5
84.	9.165	9.171	9.176	9.182	9.187	9.192	9.198	9.203	9.209	9.214	1	1	2	2	3	3	4	4	5
85.	9.220	9.225	9.230	9.236	9.241	9.247	9.252	9.257	9.263	9.268	1	1	2	2	3	3	4	4	5
86.	9.274	9.279	9.284	9.290	9.295	9.301	9.306	9.311	9.317	9.322	1	1	2	2	3	3	4	4	5
87.	9.327	9.333	9.338	9.343	9.349	9.354	9.359	9.365	9.370	9.375	1	1	2	2	3	3	4	4	5
88.	9.381	9.386	9.391	9.397	9.402	9.407	9.413	9.418	9.423	9.429	1	1	2	2	3	3	4	4	5
89.	9.434	9.439	9.445	9.450	9.455	9.460	9.466	9.471	9.476	9.482	1	1	2	2	3	3	4	4	5
90.	9.487	9.492	9.497	9.503	9.508	9.513	9.518	9.524	9.529	9.534	1	1	2	2	3	3	4	4	5
91.	9.539	9.545	9.550	9.555	9.560	9.566	9.571	9.576	9.581	9.586	1	1	2	2	3	3	4	4	5
92.	9.592	9.597	9.602	9.607	9.612	9.618	9.623	9.628	9.633	9.638	1	1	2	2	3	3	4	4	5
93.	9.644	9.649	9.654	9.659	9.664	9.670	9.675	9.680	9.685	9.690	1	1	2	2	3	3	4	4	5
94.	9.695	9.701	9.706	9.711	9.716	9.721	9.726	9.731	9.737	9.742	1	1	2	2	3	3	4	4	5
95.	9.747	9.752	9.757	9.762	9.767	9.772	9.778	9.783	9.788	9.793	1	1	2	2	3	3	4	4	5
96.	9.798	9.803	9.808	9.813	9.818	9.823	9.829	9.834	9.839	9.844	1	1	2	2	3	3	4	4	5
97.	9.849	9.854	9.859	9.864	9.869	9.874	9.879	9.884	9.889	9.894	1	1	2	2	3	3	4	4	5
98.	9.899	9.905	9.910	9.915	9.920	9.925	9.930	9.935	9.940	9.945	1	1	2	2	3	3	4	4	5
99.	9.950	9.955	9.960	9.965	9.970	9.975	9.980	9.985	9.990	9.995	1	1	2	2	3	3	4	4	5

Examples:
$$\sqrt{(862300)} = \sqrt{(86.230 \times 10^4)} = 9.286 \times 10^2 = 928.6$$
$$\sqrt{(0.0927)} = \sqrt{(9.27 \times 10^{-2})} = 3.045 \times 10^{-1} = 0.3045$$
Note that the power of 10 extracted under the root sign must always be even.

RECIPROCALS $1/x$ or x^{-1}

x	0	1	2	3	4	5	6	7	8	9	1 2 3	4 5 6	7 8 9
											1 2 3	4 5 6	SUBTRACT 7 8 9
1.00	1.0000										1 2 3	4 5 6	7 8 9
		0.9990	9980	9970	9960	9950	9940	9930	9921	9911	1 2 3	4 5 6	7 8 9
1.01	0.9901	9891	9881	9872	9862	9852	9843	9833	9823	9814	1 2 3	4 5 6	7 8 9
1.02	0.9804	9794	9785	9775	9766	9756	9747	9737	9828	9718	1 2 3	4 5 6	7 8 9
1.03	0.9709	9699	9690	9681	9671	9662	9653	9643	9634	9625	1 2 3	4 5 5	6 7 8
1.04	0.9615	9606	9597	9588	9579	9569	9560	9551	9542	9533	1 2 3	4 5 5	6 7 8
1.05	0.9524	9515	9506	9497	9488	9479	9470	9461	9452	9443	1 2 3	4 5 5	6 7 8
1.06	0.9434	9425	9416	9407	9398	9390	9381	9372	9363	9355	1 2 3	4 4 5	6 7 8
1.07	0.9346	9337	9328	9320	9311	9302	9294	9285	9276	9268	1 2 3	4 4 5	6 7 8
1.08	0.9259	9251	9242	9234	9225	9217	9208	9200	9191	9183	1 2 2	3 4 5	6 6 7
1.09	0.9174	9166	9158	9149	9141	9132	9124	9116	9107	9099	1 2 2	3 4 5	6 6 7
1.10	0.9091	9083	9074	9066	9058	9050	9042	9033	9025	9017	1 2 2	3 4 5	6 6 7
1.11	0.9009	9001	8993	8985	8977	8969	8961	8953	8945	8937	1 2 2	3 4 5	6 6 7
1.12	0.8929	8921	8913	8905	8897	8889	8881	8873	8865	8857	1 2 2	3 4 5	6 6 7
1.13	0.8850	8842	8834	8826	8818	8811	8803	8795	8787	8780	1 2 2	3 4 5	6 6 7
1.14	0.8772	8764	8757	8749	8741	8734	8726	8718	8711	8703	1 2 2	3 4 5	6 6 7
1.15	0.8696	8688	8681	8673	8666	8658	8651	8643	8636	8628	1 2 2	3 4 5	6 6 7
1.16	0.8621	8613	8606	8598	8591	8584	8576	8569	8562	8554	1 1 2	3 4 4	5 6 6
1.17	0.8547	8540	8532	8525	8518	8511	8503	8496	8489	8482	1 1 2	3 4 4	5 6 6
1.18	0.8475	8467	8460	8453	8446	8439	8432	8425	8418	8410	1 1 2	3 4 4	5 6 6
1.19	0.8403	8396	8389	8382	8375	8368	8361	8354	8347	8340	1 1 2	3 4 4	5 6 6
1.20	0.8333	8326	8319	8313	8306	8299	8292	8285	8278	8271	1 1 2	3 3 4	5 6 6
1.21	0.8264	8258	8251	8244	8237	8230	8224	8217	8210	8203	1 1 2	3 3 4	5 6 6
1.22	0.8197	8190	8183	8177	8170	8163	8157	8150	8143	8137	1 1 2	3 3 4	5 6 6
1.23	0.8130	8123	8117	8110	8104	8097	8091	8084	8078	8071	1 1 2	3 3 4	5 6 6
1.24	0.8065	8058	8052	8045	8039	8032	8026	8019	8013	8006	1 1 2	3 3 4	5 6 6
1.25	0.8000	7994	7987	7981	7974	7968	7962	7955	7949	7943	1 1 2	2 3 4	4 5 5
1.26	0.7937	7930	7924	7918	7911	7905	7899	7893	7886	7880	1 1 2	2 3 4	4 5 5
1.27	0.7874	7868	7862	7855	7849	7843	7837	7831	7825	7819	1 1 2	2 3 4	4 5 5
1.28	0.7813	7806	7800	7794	7788	7782	7776	7770	7764	7758	1 1 2	2 3 4	4 5 5
1.29	0.7752	7746	7740	7734	7728	7722	7716	7710	7704	7698	1 1 2	2 3 4	4 5 5
1.30	0.7692	7686	7680	7675	7669	7663	7657	7651	7645	7639	1 1 2	2 3 4	4 5 5
1.31	0.7634	7628	7622	7616	7610	7605	7599	7593	7587	7582	1 1 2	2 3 4	4 5 5
1.32	0.7576	7570	7564	7559	7553	7547	7541	7536	7530	7524	1 1 2	2 3 4	4 5 5
1.33	0.7519	7513	7508	7502	7496	7491	7485	7479	7474	7468	1 1 2	2 3 4	4 5 5
1.34	0.7463	7457	7452	7446	7440	7435	7429	7424	7418	7413	1 1 2	2 3 4	4 5 5
1.35	0.7407	7402	7396	7391	7386	7380	7375	7369	7364	7358	1 1 2	2 3 3	4 4 5
1.36	0.7353	7348	7342	7337	7331	7326	7321	7315	7310	7305	1 1 2	2 3 3	4 4 5
1.37	0.7299	7294	7289	7283	7278	7273	7267	7262	7257	7252	1 1 2	2 3 3	4 4 5
1.38	0.7246	7241	7236	7231	7225	7220	7215	7210	7205	7199	1 1 2	2 3 3	4 4 5
1.39	0.7194	7189	7184	7179	7174	7168	7163	7158	7153	7148	1 1 2	2 3 3	4 4 5
1.40	0.7143	7138	7133	7128	7123	7117	7112	7107	7102	7097	0 1 1	2 2 3	3 4 4
1.41	0.7092	7087	7082	7077	7072	7067	7062	7057	7052	7047	0 1 1	2 2 3	3 4 4
1.42	0.7042	7037	7032	7027	7022	7018	7013	7008	7003	6998	0 1 1	2 2 3	3 4 4
1.43	0.6993	6988	6983	6978	6974	6969	6964	6959	6954	6949	0 1 1	2 2 3	3 4 4
1.44	0.6944	6940	6935	6930	6925	6920	6916	6911	6906	6901	0 1 1	2 2 3	3 4 4
1.45	0.6897	6892	6887	6882	6878	6873	6868	6863	6859	6854	0 1 1	2 2 3	3 4 4
1.46	0.6849	6845	6840	6835	6831	6826	6821	6817	6812	6807	0 1 1	2 2 3	3 4 4
1.47	0.6803	6798	6793	6789	6784	6780	6775	6770	6766	6761	0 1 1	2 2 3	3 4 4
1.48	0.6757	6752	6748	6743	6739	6734	6729	6725	6720	6716	0 1 1	2 2 3	3 4 4
1.49	0.6711	6707	6702	6698	6693	6689	6684	6680	6676	6671	0 1 1	2 2 2	3 3 4

Examples:

$$(163.7)^{-1} = (1.637 \times 10^2)^{-1} = 0.6108 \times 10^{-2}$$
$$(0.006108)^{-1} = (6.108 \times 10^{-3})^{-1} = 0.1637 \times 10^3$$

It is sometimes more accurate to use:

$$1/x = \tfrac{1}{2} \times 1/(\tfrac{1}{2}x) \quad \text{or} \quad 1/x = 2 \times 1/(2x)$$

Thus $1/9.3 = 2 \times 1/18.6 = 2 \times 0.05376 = 0.10752$ with an error of at most 1 in the last place.

RECIPROCALS $1/x$ or x^{-1}

x	0	1	2	3	4	5	6	7	8	9	1 2 3	4 5 6	7 8 9
												SUBTRACT	
1.5	0.6667	6623	6579	6536	6494	6452					4 9 13	17 21 26	30 34 39
							6410	6369	6329	6289	4 8 12	16 20 24	28 32 36
1.6	0.6250	6211	6173	6135	6098						4 8 11	15 19 23	27 30 34
						6061	6024	5988	5952	5917	4 7 11	14 18 22	25 29 32
1.7	0.5882	5848	5814	5780	5747						3 7 10	14 17 20	24 27 31
						5714	5682	5650	5618	5587	3 6 10	13 16 19	22 26 29
1.8	0.5556	5525	5495	5464	5435						3 6 9	12 15 18	21 24 27
						5405	5376	5348	5319	5291	3 6 8	11 14 17	20 22 25
1.9	0.5263	5236	5208	5181	5155						3 5 8	11 14 16	19 22 24
						5128	5102	5076	5051	5025	3 5 8	10 13 16	18 21 23
2.0	0.5000	4975	4950	4926	4902	4878	4854	4831	4808	4785	2 5 7	10 12 14	17 19 22
2.1	0.4762	4739	4717	4695	4673	4651	4630	4608	4587	4566	2 4 7	9 11 13	15 18 20
2.2	0.4545	4525	4505	4484	4464	4444	4425	4405	4386	4367	2 4 6	8 10 12	14 16 18
2.3	0.4348	4329	4310	4292	4274	4255	4237	4219	4202	4184	2 4 5	7 9 11	13 14 16
2.4	0.4167	4149	4132	4115	4098	4082	4065	4049	4032	4016	2 3 5	7 8 10	12 14 15
2.5	0.4000	3984	3968	3953	3937	3922	3906	3891	3876	3861	2 3 5	6 8 9	11 12 14
2.6	0.3846	3831	3817	3802	3788	3774	3759	3745	3731	3717	1 3 4	6 7 8	10 11 13
2.7	0.3704	3690	3676	3663	3650	3636	3623	3610	3597	3584	1 3 4	5 7 8	9 11 12
2.8	0.3571	3559	3546	3534	3521	3509	3497	3484	3472	3460	1 2 4	5 6 7	9 10 11
2.9	0.3448	3436	3425	3413	3401	3390	3378	3367	3356	3344	1 2 3	5 6 7	8 9 10
3.0	0.3333	3322	3311	3300	3289	3279	3268	3257	3247	3236	1 2 3	4 5 6	8 9 10
3.1	0.3226	3215	3205	3195	3185	3175	3165	3155	3145	3135	1 2 3	4 5 6	7 8 9
3.2	0.3125	3115	3106	3096	3086	3077	3067	3058	3049	3040	1 2 3	4 5 6	7 8 9
3.3	0.3030	3021	3012	3003	2994	2985	2976	2967	2959	2950	1 2 3	4 4 5	6 7 8
3.4	0.2941	2933	2924	2915	2907	2899	2890	2882	2874	2865	1 2 3	3 4 5	6 7 8
3.5	0.2857	2849	2841	2833	2825	2817	2809	2801	2793	2786	1 2 2	3 4 5	6 6 7
3.6	0.2778	2770	2762	2755	2747	2740	2732	2725	2717	2710	1 2 2	3 4 5	5 6 7
3.7	0.2703	2695	2688	2681	2674	2667	2660	2653	2646	2639	1 1 2	3 4 4	5 6 6
3.8	0.2632	2625	2618	2611	2604	2597	2591	2584	2577	2571	1 1 2	3 3 4	5 5 6
3.9	0.2564	2558	2551	2545	2538	2532	2525	2519	2513	2506	1 1 2	3 3 4	4 5 6
4.0	0.2500	2494	2488	2481	2475	2469	2463	2457	2451	2445	1 1 2	2 3 4	4 5 6
4.1	0.2439	2433	2427	2421	2415	2410	2404	2398	2392	2387	1 1 2	2 3 3	4 5 5
4.2	0.2381	2375	2370	2364	2358	2353	2347	2342	2336	2331	1 1 2	2 3 3	4 4 5
4.3	0.2326	2320	2315	2309	2304	2299	2294	2288	2283	2278	1 1 2	2 3 3	4 4 5
4.4	0.2273	2268	2262	2257	2252	2247	2242	2237	2232	2227	1 1 2	2 3 3	4 4 5
4.5	0.2222	2217	2212	2208	2203	2198	2193	2188	2183	2179	0 1 1	2 2 3	3 4 4
4.6	0.2174	2169	2165	2160	2155	2151	2146	2141	2137	2132	0 1 1	2 2 3	3 4 4
4.7	0.2128	2123	2119	2114	2110	2105	2101	2096	2092	2088	0 1 1	2 2 3	3 4 4
4.8	0.2083	2079	2075	2070	2066	2062	2058	2053	2049	2045	0 1 1	2 2 3	3 3 4
4.9	0.2041	2037	2033	2028	2024	2020	2016	2012	2008	2004	0 1 1	2 2 2	3 3 4
5.0	0.2000	1996	1992	1988	1984	1980	1976	1972	1969	1965	0 1 1	2 2 2	3 3 4
5.1	0.1961	1957	1953	1949	1946	1942	1938	1934	1931	1927	0 1 1	2 2 2	3 3 3
5.2	0.1923	1919	1916	1912	1908	1905	1901	1898	1894	1890	0 1 1	1 2 2	3 3 3
5.3	0.1887	1883	1880	1876	1873	1869	1866	1862	1859	1855	0 1 1	1 2 2	2 3 3
5.4	0.1852	1848	1845	1842	1838	1835	1832	1828	1825	1821	0 1 1	1 2 2	2 3 3
5.5	0.1818	1815	1812	1808	1805	1802	1799	1795	1792	1789	0 1 1	1 2 2	2 3 3
5.6	0.1786	1783	1779	1776	1773	1770	1767	1764	1761	1757	0 1 1	1 2 2	2 3 3
5.7	0.1754	1751	1748	1745	1742	1739	1736	1733	1730	1727	0 1 1	1 2 2	2 2 3
5.8	0.1724	1721	1718	1715	1712	1709	1706	1704	1701	1698	0 1 1	1 1 2	2 2 3
5.9	0.1695	1692	1689	1686	1684	1681	1678	1675	1672	1669	0 1 1	1 1 2	2 2 3
6.	0.1667	1639	1613								3 5 8	11 13 16	19 22 24
				1587	1563	1538					2 5 7	10 12 14	17 19 22
							1515	1493	1471	1449	2 4 6	8 11 13	15 17 19
7.	0.1429	1408	1389	1370							2 4 6	8 10 12	14 16 18
					1351	1333	1316	1299	1282	1266	2 3 5	7 9 10	12 14 15
8.	0.1250	1235	1220	1205							2 3 5	6 8 9	11 12 14
					1190	1176	1163	1149	1136	1124	1 3 4	5 7 8	9 10 12
9.	0.1111	1099	1087	1075	1064	1053	1042	1031	1020	1010	1 2 3	4 6 7	8 9 10

POWERS AND FACTORIALS

x	x^2	x^3	$10/x$	$\sqrt{x}$	$1/\sqrt{x}$	$\sqrt[3]{x}$ Δ	$\sqrt[3]{(10x)}$ Δ	$\sqrt[3]{(100x)}$ Δ	$x!$	lg $x!$
						+	+	+	§	
1	1	1	10	1.000	1.0000	1.000	2.154	4.642	1	0
2	4	8	5	1.414	0.7071	1.260 *	2.714 *	5.848 *	2	0.3010
3	9	27	3.333	1.732	.5774	1.442	3.107	6.694	6	0.7782
4	16	64	2.5	2.000	.5000	1.587	3.420	7.368	24	1.3802
5	25	125	2	2.236	.4472	1.710	3.684	7.937	120	2.0792
6	36	216	1.667	2.449	.4082	1.817	3.915	8.434	720	2.8573
7	49	343	1.429	2.646	.3780	1.913	4.121	8.879	5040	3.7024
8	64	512	1.25	2.828	.3536	2.000	4.309	9.283	4.032	4.6055
9	81	729	1.111	3.000	.3333	2.080	4.481	9.655	3.629	5.5598
10	1 00	1 000	1	3.162	.3162	2.154 70	4.642 149†	10.00 32	3.629	6.5598
11	1 21	1 331	.9091	3.317	.3015	2.224 65	4.791 141†	10.32 31	3.992	7.6012
12	1 44	1 728	.8333	3.464	.2887	2.289 62	4.932 134†	10.63 28	4.790	8.6803
13	1 69	2 197	.7692	3.606	.2774	2.351 59	5.066 126	10.91 28	6.227	9.7943
14	1 96	2 744	.7143	3.742	.2673	2.410 56	5.192 121	11.19 26	8.718	10.9404
15	2 25	3 375	.6667	3.873	.2582	2.466 54	5.313 116	11.45 25	1.308	12.1165
16	2 56	4 096	.6250	4.000	.2500	2.520 51	5.429 111	11.70 23	2.092	13.3206
17	2 89	4 913	.5882	4.123	.2425	2.571 50	5.540 106	11.93 23	3.557	14.5511
18	3 24	5 832	.5556	4.243	.2357	2.621 47	5.646 103	12.16 23	6.402	15.8063
19	3 61	6 859	.5263	4.359	.2294	2.668 46	5.749 99	12.39 21	1.216	17.0851
20	4 00	8 000	.5000	4.472	.2236	2.714 45	5.848 96	12.60 21	2.433	18.3861
21	4 41	9 261	.4762	4.583	.2182	2.759 43	5.944 93	12.81 20	5.109	19.7083
22	4 84	10 648	.4545	4.690	.2132	2.802 42	6.037 90	13.01 19	1.124	21.0508
23	5 29	12 167	.4348	4.796	.2085	2.844 40	6.127 87	13.20 19	2.585	22.4125
24	5 76	13 824	.4167	4.899	.2041	2.884 40	6.214 86	13.39 18	6.204	23.7927
25	6 25	15 625	.4000	5.000	.2000	2.924 38	6.300 83	13.57 18	1.551	25.1906
26	6 76	17 576	.3846	5.099	.1961	2.962 38	6.383 80	13.75 17	4.033	26.6056
27	7 29	19 683	.3704	5.196	.1925	3.000 37	6.463 79	13.92 17	1.089	28.0370
28	7 84	21 952	.3571	5.292	.1890	3.037 35	6.542 77	14.09 17	3.049	29.4841
29	8 41	24 389	.3448	5.385	.1857	3.072 35	6.619 75	14.26 16	8.842	30.9465
30	9 00	27 000	.3333	5.477	.1826	3.107 34	6.694 74	14.42 16	2.653	32.4237
31	9 61	29 791	.3226	5.568	.1796	3.141 34	6.768 72	14.58 16	8.223	33.9150
32	10 24	32 768	.3125	5.657	.1768	3.175 33	6.840 70	14.74 15	2.631	35.4202
33	10 89	35 937	.3030	5.745	.1741	3.208 32	6.910 70	14.89 15	8.683	36.9387
34	11 56	39 304	.2941	5.831	.1715	3.240 31	6.980 67	15.04 14	2.952	38.4702
35	12 25	42 875	.2857	5.916	.1690	3.271 31	7.047 67	15.18 15	1.033	40.0142
36	12 96	46 656	.2778	6.000	.1667	3.302 30	7.114 65	15.33 14	3.720	41.5705
37	13 69	50 653	.2703	6.083	.1644	3.332 30	7.179 64	15.47 13	1.376	43.1387
38	14 44	54 872	.2632	6.164	.1622	3.362 29	7.243 63	15.60 14	5.230	44.7185
39	15 21	59 319	.2564	6.245	.1601	3.391 29	7.306 62	15.74 13	2.040	46.3096
40	16 00	64 000	.2500	6.325	.1581	3.420 28	7.368 61	15.87 14	8.159	47.9116
41	16 81	68 921	.2439	6.403	.1562	3.448 28	7.429 60	16.01 12	3.345	49.5244
42	17 64	74 088	.2381	6.481	.1543	3.476 27	7.489 59	16.13 13	1.405	51.1477
43	18 49	79 507	.2326	6.557	.1525	3.503 27	7.548 58	16.26 13	6.042	52.7811
44	19 36	85 184	.2273	6.633	.1508	3.530 27	7.606 57	16.39 12	2.658	54.4246
45	20 25	91 125	.2222	6.708	.1491	3.557 26	7.663 56	16.51 12	1.196	56.0778
46	21 16	97 336	.2174	6.782	.1474	3.583 26	7.719 56	16.63 12	5.503	57.7406
47	22 09	103 823	.2128	6.856	.1459	3.609 25	7.775 55	16.75 12	2.586	59.4127
48	23 04	110 592	.2083	6.928	.1443	3.634 25	7.830 54	16.87 11	1.241	61.0939
49	24 01	117 649	.2041	7.000	.1429	3.659 25	7.884 53	16.98 12	6.083	62.7841

* To interpolate in the interval $1 < x < 10$, put $y = 10x$, and use the relations $\sqrt[3]{x} = \frac{1}{10}\sqrt[3]{(100y)}$, $\sqrt[3]{(10x)} = \sqrt[3]{y}$, $\sqrt[3]{(100x)} = \sqrt[3]{(10y)}$.

Example: $\sqrt[3]{(3.4)} = \frac{1}{10}\sqrt[3]{(100 \times 34)} = \frac{1}{10} \times 15.04 = 1.504$

† For $10 < x < 13$ errors of linear interpolation may amount to 2 units in the third decimal place.

§ For $x \geqslant 8$ multiply by 10^c, where c is the integer part (*characteristic*) of lg $x!$.
Example: $28! = 3.049 \times 10^{29}$ to 4 significant figures.

POWERS AND FACTORIALS

x	x^2	x^3	$10/x$	$\sqrt{x}$	$1/\sqrt{x}$	$\sqrt[3]{x}$	Δ	$\sqrt[3]{(10x)}$	Δ	$\sqrt[3]{(100x)}$	Δ	$x!$	lg $x!$
							+		+		+	§	
50	25 00	125 000	.2000	7.071	.1414	3.684	24	7.937	53	17.10	11	3.041	64.4831
51	26 01	132 651	.1961	7.141	.1400	3.708	25	7.990	51	17.21	11	1.551	66.1906
52	27 04	140 608	.1923	7.211	.1387	3.733	23	8.041	52	17.32	12	8.066	67.9066
53	28 09	148 877	.1887	7.280	.1374	3.756	24	8.093	50	17.44	10	4.275	69.6309
54	29 16	157 464	.1852	7.348	.1361	3.780	23	8.143	50	17.54	11	2.308	71.3633
55	30 25	166 375	.1818	7.416	.1348	3.803	23	8.193	50	17.65	11	1.270	73.1037
56	31 36	175 616	.1786	7.483	.1336	3.826	23	8.243	48	17.76	10	7.110	74.8519
57	32 49	185 193	.1754	7.550	.1325	3.849	22	8.291	49	17.86	11	4.053	76.6077
58	33 64	195 112	.1724	7.616	.1313	3.871	22	8.340	47	17.97	10	2.351	78.3712
59	34 81	205 379	.1695	7.681	.1302	3.893	22	8.387	47	18.07	10	1.387	80.1420
60	36 00	216 000	.1667	7.746	.1291	3.915	21	8.434	47	18.17	10	8.321	81.9202
61	37 21	226 981	.1639	7.810	.1280	3.936	22	8.481	46	18.27	10	5.076	83.7055
62	38 44	238 328	.1613	7.874	.1270	3.958	21	8.527	46	18.37	10	3.147	85.4979
63	39 69	250 047	.1587	7.937	.1260	3.979	21	8.573	45	18.47	10	1.983	87.2972
64	40 96	262 144	.1562	8.000	.1250	4.000	21	8.618	44	18.57	9	1.269	89.1034
65	42 25	274 625	.1538	8.062	.1240	4.021	20	8.662	45	18.66	10	8.248	90.9163
66	43 56	287 496	.1515	8.124	.1231	4.041	21	8.707	43	18.76	9	5.443	92.7359
67	44 89	300 763	.1493	8.185	.1222	4.062	20	8.750	44	18.85	10	3.647	94.5619
68	46 24	314 432	.1471	8.246	.1213	4.082	20	8.794	43	18.95	9	2.480	96.3945
69	47 61	328 509	.1449	8.307	.1204	4.102	19	8.837	42	19.04	9	1.711	98.2333
70	49 00	343 000	.1429	8.367	.1195	4.121	20	8.879	42	19.13	9	1.198	100.0784
71	50 41	357 911	.1408	8.426	.1187	4.141	19	8.921	42	19.22	9	8.505	101.9297
72	51 84	373 248	.1389	8.485	.1179	4.160	19	8.963	41	19.31	9	6.123	103.7870
73	53 29	389 017	.1370	8.544	.1170	4.179	19	9.004	41	19.40	9	4.470	105.6503
74	54 76	405 224	.1351	8.602	.1162	4.198	19	9.045	41	19.49	8	3.308	107.5196
75	56 25	421 875	.1333	8.660	.1155	4.217	19	9.086	40	19.57	9	2.481	109.3946
76	57 76	438 976	.1316	8.718	.1147	4.236	18	9.126	40	19.66	9	1.885	111.2754
77	59 29	456 533	.1299	8.775	.1140	4.254	19	9.166	39	19.75	8	1.452	113.1619
78	60 84	474 552	.1282	8.832	.1132	4.273	18	9.205	39	19.83	9	1.132	115.0540
79	62 41	493 039	.1266	8.888	.1125	4.291	18	9.244	39	19.92	8	8.946	116.9516
80	64 00	512 000	.1250	8.944	.1118	4.309	18	9.283	39	20.00	8	7.157	118.8547
81	65 61	531 441	.1235	9.000	.1111	4.327	17	9.322	38	20.08	9	5.797	120.7632
82	67 24	551 368	.1220	9.055	.1104	4.344	18	9.360	38	20.17	8	4.754	122.6770
83	68 89	571 787	.1205	9.110	.1098	4.362	18	9.398	37	20.25	8	3.946	124.5961
84	70 56	592 704	.1190	9.165	.1091	4.380	17	9.435	38	20.33	8	3.314	126.5204
85	72 25	614 125	.1176	9.220	.1085	4.397	17	9.473	37	20.41	8	2.817	128.4498
86	73 96	636 056	.1163	9.274	.1078	4.414	17	9.510	36	20.49	8	2.423	130.3843
87	75 69	658 503	.1149	9.327	.1072	4.431	17	9.546	37	20.57	8	2.108	132.3238
88	77 44	681 472	.1136	9.381	.1066	4.448	17	9.583	36	20.65	7	1.855	134.2683
89	79 21	704 969	.1124	9.434	.1060	4.465	16	9.619	36	20.72	8	1.651	136.2177
90	81 00	729 000	.1111	9.487	.1054	4.481	17	9.655	36	20.80	8	1.486	138.1719
91	82 81	753 571	.1099	9.539	.1048	4.498	16	9.691	35	20.88	7	1.352	140.1310
92	84 64	778 688	.1087	9.592	.1043	4.514	17	9.726	35	20.95	8	1.244	142.0948
93	86 49	804 357	.1075	9.644	.1037	4.531	16	9.761	35	21.03	7	1.157	144.0632
94	88 36	830 584	.1064	9.695	.1031	4.547	16	9.796	34	21.10	8	1.087	146.0364
95	90 25	857 375	.1053	9.747	.1026	4.563	16	9.830	35	21.18	7	1.033	148.0141
96	92 16	884 736	.1042	9.798	.1021	4.579	16	9.865	34	21.25	8	9.917	149.9964
97	94 09	912 673	.1031	9.849	.1015	4.595	15	9.899	34	21.33	7	9.619	151.9831
98	96 04	941 192	.1020	9.899	.1010	4.610	16	9.933	34	21.40	7	9.427	153.9744
99	98 01	970 299	.1010	9.950	.1005	4.626	16	9.967	33	21.47	7	9.333	155.9700
100	10^4	10^6	.1000	10	.1000	4.642		10		21.54		9.333	157.9700

§ Multiply by 10^c, where c is the integer part (*characteristic*) of lg $x!$.

Example: 70! $= 1.198 \times 10^{100}$ to 4 significant figures.

	0' 0°.0	6' 0°.1	12' 0°.2	18' 0°.3	24' 0°.4	30' 0°.5	36' 0°.6	42' 0°.7	48' 0°.8	54' 0°.9	1'	2'	3'	4'	5' ADD
0°	0.0000	0017	0035	0052	0070	0087	0105	0122	0140	0157	3	6	9	12	15
1	0.0175	0192	0209	0227	0244	0262	0279	0297	0314	0332	3	6	9	12	15
2	0.0349	0367	0384	0401	0419	0436	0454	0471	0489	0.506	3	6	9	12	15
3	0.0524	0541	0559	0576	0593	0611	0628	0646	0663	0681	3	6	9	12	15
4	0.0698	0716	0733	0750	0768	0785	0803	0820	0838	0855	3	6	9	12	15
5	0.0873	0890	0908	0925	0942	0960	0977	0995	1012	1030	3	6	9	12	15
6	0.1047	1065	1082	1100	1117	1134	1152	1169	1187	1204	3	6	9	12	15
7	0.1222	1239	1257	1274	1292	1309	1326	1344	1361	1379	3	6	9	12	15
8	0.1396	1414	1431	1449	1466	1484	1501	1518	1536	1553	3	6	9	12	15
9	0.1571	1588	1606	1623	1641	1658	1676	1693	1710	1728	3	6	9	12	15
10	0.1745	1763	1780	1798	1815	1833	1850	1868	1885	1902	3	6	9	12	15
11	0.1920	1937	1955	1972	1990	2007	2025	2042	2060	2077	3	6	9	12	15
12	0.2094	2112	2129	2147	2164	2182	2199	2217	2234	2251	3	6	9	12	15
13	0.2269	2286	2304	2321	2339	2356	2374	2391	2409	2426	3	6	9	12	15
14	0.2443	2461	2478	2496	2513	2531	2548	2566	2583	2601	3	6	9	12	15
15	0.2618	2635	2653	2670	2688	2705	2723	2740	2758	2775	3	6	9	12	15
16	0.2793	2810	2827	2845	2862	2880	2897	2915	2932	2950	3	6	9	12	15
17	0.2967	2985	3002	3019	3037	3054	3072	3089	3107	3124	3	6	9	12	15
18	0.3142	3159	3176	3194	3211	3229	3246	3264	3281	3299	3	6	9	12	15
19	0.3316	3334	3351	3368	3386	3403	3421	3438	3456	3473	3	6	9	12	15
20	0.3491	3508	3526	3543	3560	3578	3595	3613	3630	3648	3	6	9	12	15
21	0.3665	3683	3700	3718	3735	3752	3770	3787	3805	3822	3	6	9	12	15
22	0.3840	3857	3875	3892	3910	3927	3944	3962	3979	3997	3	6	9	12	15
23	0.4014	4032	4049	4067	4084	4102	4119	4136	4154	4171	3	6	9	12	15
24	0.4189	4206	4224	4241	4259	4276	4294	4311	4328	4346	3	6	9	12	15
25	0.4363	4381	4398	4416	4433	4451	4468	4485	4503	4520	3	6	9	12	15
26	0.4538	4555	4573	4590	4608	4625	4643	4660	4677	4695	3	6	9	12	15
27	0.4712	4730	4747	4765	4782	4800	4817	4835	4852	4869	3	6	9	12	15
28	0.4887	4904	4922	4939	4957	4974	4992	5009	5027	5044	3	6	9	12	15
29	0.5061	5079	5096	5114	5131	5149	5166	5184	5201	5219	3	6	9	12	15
30	0.5236	5253	5271	5288	5306	5323	5341	5358	5376	5393	3	6	9	12	15
31	0.5411	5428	5445	5463	5480	5498	5515	5533	5550	5568	3	6	9	12	15
32	0.5585	5603	5620	5637	5655	5672	5690	5707	5725	5742	3	6	9	12	15
33	0.5760	5777	5794	5812	5829	5847	5864	5882	5899	5917	3	6	9	12	15
34	0.5934	5952	5969	5986	6004	6021	6039	6056	6074	6091	3	6	9	12	15
35	0.6109	6126	6144	6161	6178	6196	6213	6231	6248	6266	3	6	9	12	15
36	0.6283	6301	6318	6336	6353	6370	6388	6405	6423	6440	3	6	9	12	15
37	0.6458	6475	6493	6510	6528	6545	6562	6580	6597	6615	3	6	9	12	15
38	0.6632	6650	6667	6685	6702	6720	6737	6754	6772	6789	3	6	9	12	15
39	0.6807	6824	6842	6859	6877	6894	6912	6929	6946	6964	3	6	9	12	15
40	0.6981	6999	7016	7034	7051	7069	7086	7103	7121	7138	3	6	9	12	15
41	0.7156	7173	7191	7208	7226	7243	7261	7278	7295	7313	3	6	9	12	15
42	0.7330	7348	7365	7383	7400	7418	7435	7453	7470	7487	1	6	9	12	15
43	0.7505	7522	7540	7557	7575	7592	7610	7627	7645	7662	3	6	9	12	15
44	0.7679	7697	7714	7732	7749	7767	7784	7802	7819	7837	3	6	9	12	15
45	0.7854	7871	7889	7906	7924	7941	7959	7976	7994	8011	3	6	9	12	15
46	0.8029	8046	8063	8081	8098	8116	8133	8151	8168	8186	3	6	9	12	15
47	0.8203	8221	8238	8255	8273	8290	8308	8325	8343	8360	3	6	9	12	15
48	0.8378	8395	8412	8430	8447	8465	8482	8500	8517	8535	3	6	9	12	15
49	0.8552	8570	8587	8604	8622	8639	8657	8674	8692	8709	3	6	9	12	15
50	0.8727	8744	8762	8779	8796	8814	8831	8849	8866	8884	3	6	9	12	15
51	0.8901	8919	8936	8954	8971	8988	9006	9023	9041	9058	3	6	9	12	15
52	0.9076	9093	9111	9128	9146	9163	9180	9198	9215	9233	3	6	9	12	15
53	0.9250	9268	9285	9303	9320	9338	9355	9372	9390	9407	3	6	9	12	15
54	0.9425	9442	9460	9477	9495	9512	9529	9547	9564	9582	3	6	9	12	15

DEGREES AND MINUTES TO RADIANS

	0' 0°.0	6' 0°.1	12' 0°.2	18' 0°.3	24' 0°.4	30' 0°.5	36' 0°.6	42' 0°.7	48' 0°.8	54' 0°.9	1'	2'	3'	4'	5' ADD
55°	0.9599	9617	9634	9652	9669	9687	9704	9721	9739	9756	3	6	9	12	15
56	0.9774	9791	9809	9826	9844	9861	9879	9896	9913	9931	3	6	9	12	15
57	0.9948	9966	9983	1.0001	0018	0036	0053	0071	0088	0105	3	6	9	12	15
58	1.0123	0140	0158	0175	0193	0210	0228	0245	0263	0280	3	6	9	12	15
59	1.0297	0315	0332	0350	0367	0385	0402	0420	0437	0455	3	6	9	12	15
60	1.0472	0489	0507	0524	0542	0559	0577	0594	0612	0629	3	6	9	12	15
61	1.0647	0664	0681	0699	0716	0734	0751	0769	0786	0804	3	6	9	12	15
62	1.0821	0838	0856	0873	0891	0908	0926	0943	0961	0978	3	6	9	12	15
63	1.0996	1013	1030	1048	1065	1083	1100	1118	1135	1153	3	6	9	12	15
64	1.1170	1188	1205	1222	1240	1257	1275	1292	1310	1327	3	6	9	12	15
65	1.1345	1362	1380	1397	1414	1432	1449	1467	1484	1502	3	6	9	12	15
66	1.1519	1537	1554	1572	1589	1606	1624	1641	1659	1676	3	6	9	12	15
67	1.1694	1711	1729	1746	1764	1781	1798	1816	1833	1851	3	6	9	12	15
68	1.1868	1886	1903	1921	1938	1956	1973	1990	2008	2025	3	6	9	12	15
69	1.2043	2060	2078	2095	2113	2130	2147	2165	2182	2200	3	6	9	12	15
70	1.2217	2235	2252	2270	2287	2305	2322	2339	2357	2374	3	6	9	12	15
71	1.2392	2409	2427	2444	2462	2479	2497	2514	2531	2549	3	6	9	12	15
72	1.2566	2584	2601	2619	2636	2654	2671	2689	2706	2723	3	6	9	12	15
73	1.2741	2758	2776	2793	2811	2828	2846	2863	2881	2898	3	6	9	12	15
74	1.2915	2933	2950	2968	2985	3003	3020	3038	3055	3073	3	6	9	12	15
75	1.3090	3107	3125	3142	3160	3177	3195	3212	3230	3247	3	6	9	12	15
76	1.3265	3282	3299	3317	3334	3352	3369	3387	3404	3422	3	6	9	12	15
77	1.3439	3456	3474	3491	3509	3526	3544	3561	3579	3596	3	6	9	12	15
78	1.3614	3631	3648	3666	3683	3701	3718	3736	3753	3771	3	6	9	12	15
79	1.3788	3806	3823	3840	3858	3875	3893	3910	3928	3945	3	6	9	12	15
80	1.3963	3980	3998	4015	4032	4050	4067	4085	4102	4120	3	6	9	12	15
81	1.4137	4155	4172	4190	4207	4224	4242	4259	4277	4294	3	6	9	12	15
82	1.4312	4329	4347	4364	4382	4399	4416	4434	4451	4469	3	6	9	12	15
83	1.4486	4504	4521	4539	4556	4573	4591	4608	4626	4643	3	6	9	12	15
84	1.4661	4678	4696	4713	4731	4748	4765	4783	4800	4818	3	6	9	12	15
85	1.4835	4853	4870	4888	4905	4923	4940	4957	4975	4992	3	6	9	12	15
86	1.5010	5027	5045	5062	5080	5097	5115	5132	5149	5167	3	6	9	12	15
87	1.5184	5202	5219	5237	5254	5272	5289	5307	5324	5341	3	6	9	12	15
88	1.5359	5376	5394	5411	5429	5446	5464	5481	5499	5516	3	6	9	12	15
89	1.5533	5551	5568	5586	5603	5621	5638	5656	5673	5691	3	6	9	12	15

RADIANS TO DEGREES

rad	0.00	0.01	0.02	0.03	0.04	0.05	0.06	0.07	0.08	0.09	1	2	3	4	5	6	7	8	9 ADD
0.0	0°.00	0.57	1.15	1.72	2.29	2.86	3.44	4.01	4.58	5.16	6	11	17	23	29	34	40	46	52
0.1	5°.73	6.30	6.88	7.45	8.02	8.59	9.17	9.74	10.31	10.89	6	11	17	23	29	34	40	46	52
0.2	11°.46	12.03	12.61	13.18	13.75	14.32	14.90	15.47	16.04	16.62	6	11	17	23	29	34	40	46	52
0.3	17°.19	17.76	18.33	18.91	19.48	20.05	20.63	21.20	21.77	22.35	6	11	17	23	29	34	40	46	52
0.4	22°.92	23.49	24.06	24.64	25.21	25.78	26.36	26.93	27.50	28.07	6	11	17	23	29	34	40	46	52
0.5	28°.65	29.22	29.79	30.37	30.94	31.51	32.09	32.66	33.23	33.80	6	11	17	23	29	34	40	46	52
0.6	34°.38	34.95	35.52	36.10	36.67	37.24	37.82	38.39	38.96	39.53	6	11	17	23	29	34	40	46	52
0.7	40°.11	40.68	41.25	41.83	42.40	42.97	43.54	44.12	44.69	45.26	6	11	17	23	29	34	40	46	52
0.8	45°.84	46.41	46.98	47.56	48.13	48.70	49.27	49.85	50.42	50.99	6	11	17	23	29	34	40	46	52
0.9	51°.57	52.14	52.71	53.29	53.86	54.43	55.00	55.58	56.15	56.72	6	11	17	23	29	34	40	46	52

rad	1	2	3	4	5	6	7	8	9	10
deg.	57°.30	114°.59	171°.89	229°.18	286°.48	343°.77	401°.07	458°.37	515°.66	572°.96

NATURAL LOGARITHMS   ln x or log$_e$ x

x	0	1	2	3	4	5	6	7	8	9
1.0	0.0000	0100	0198	0296	0392	0488	0583	0677	0770	0862
1.1	0.0953	1044	1133	1222	1310	1398	1484	1570	1655	1740
1.2	0.1823	1906	1989	2070	2151	2231	2311	2390	2469	2546
1.3	0.2624	2700	2776	2852	2927	3001	3075	3148	3221	3293
1.4	0.3365	3436	3507	3577	3646	3716	3784	3853	3920	3988
1.5	0.4055	4121	4187	4253	4318	4383	4447	4511	4574	4637
1.6	0.4700	4762	4824	4886	4947	5008	5068	5128	5188	5247
1.7	0.5306	5365	5423	5481	5539	5596	5653	5710	5766	5822
1.8	0.5878	5933	5988	6043	6098	6152	6206	6259	6313	6366
1.9	0.6419	6471	6523	6575	6627	6678	6729	6780	6831	6881
2.0	0.6931	6981	7031	7080	7129	7178	7227	7275	7324	7372
2.1	0.7419	7467	7514	7561	7608	7655	7701	7747	7793	7839
2.2	0.7885	7930	7975	8020	8065	8109	8154	8198	8242	8286
2.3	0.8329	8372	8416	8459	8502	8544	8587	8629	8671	8713
2.4	0.8755	8796	8838	8879	8920	8961	9002	9042	9083	9123
2.5	0.9163	9203	9243	9282	9322	9361	9400	9439	9478	9517
2.6	0.9555	9594	9632	9670	9708	9746	9783	9821	9858	9895
2.7	0.9933	9969	1.0006	0043	0080	0116	0152	0188	0225	0260
2.8	1.0296	0332	0367	0403	0438	0473	0508	0543	0578	0613
2.9	1.0647	0682	0716	0750	0784	0818	0852	0886	0919	0953
3.0	1.0986	1019	1053	1086	1119	1151	1184	1217	1249	1282
3.1	1.1314	1346	1378	1410	1442	1474	1506	1537	1569	1600
3.2	1.1632	1663	1694	1725	1756	1787	1817	1848	1878	1909
3.3	1.1939	1969	2000	2030	2060	2090	2119	2149	2179	2208
3.4	1.2238	2267	2296	2326	2355	2384	2413	2442	2470	2499
3.5	1.2528	2556	2585	2613	2641	2669	2698	2726	2754	2782
3.6	1.2809	2837	2865	2892	2920	2947	2975	3002	3029	3056
3.7	1.3083	3110	3137	3164	3191	3218	3244	3271	3297	3324
3.8	1.3350	3376	3403	3429	3455	3481	3507	3533	3558	3584
3.9	1.3610	3635	3661	3686	3712	3737	3762	3788	3813	3838
4.0	1.3863	3888	3913	3938	3962	3987	4012	4036	4061	4085
4.1	1.4110	4134	4159	4183	4207	4231	4255	4279	4303	4327
4.2	1.4351	4375	4398	4422	4446	4469	4493	4516	4540	4563
4.3	1.4586	4609	4633	4656	4679	4702	4725	4748	4770	4793
4.4	1.4816	4839	4861	4884	4907	4929	4951	4974	4996	5019
4.5	1.5041	5063	5085	5107	5129	5151	5173	5195	5217	5239
4.6	1.5261	5282	5304	5326	5347	5369	5390	5412	5433	5454
4.7	1.5476	5497	5518	5539	5560	5581	5602	5623	5644	5665
4.8	1.5686	5707	5728	5748	5769	5790	5810	5831	5851	5872
4.9	1.5892	5913	5933	5953	5974	5994	6014	6034	6054	6074

ADD (proportional parts)

x	1	2	3	4	5	6	7	8	9
1.0	10	20	30	40	49	59	69	79	89
	10	19	29	38	48	57	67	76	86
	9	18	28	37	46	55	64	74	83
1.1	9	18	27	36	45	54	63	72	81
	9	17	26	35	44	52	61	70	78
	8	17	25	34	42	50	59	67	76
1.2	8	16	25	33	41	49	57	66	74
	8	16	24	32	40	48	56	64	72
	8	16	23	31	39	47	55	62	70
1.3	8	15	23	30	38	45	53	60	68
	7	15	22	29	36	44	51	58	66
1.4	7	14	21	28	35	42	49	56	63
	7	14	20	27	34	41	48	54	61
1.5	7	13	20	26	33	40	46	53	59
	6	13	19	25	32	38	44	50	57
1.6	6	12	19	25	31	37	43	50	56
	6	12	18	24	30	36	42	48	54
1.7	6	12	17	23	29	35	41	46	52
	6	11	17	22	28	34	39	45	50
1.8	5	11	16	22	27	32	38	43	49
1.9	5	10	15	20	26	31	36	41	46
2.0	5	10	15	20	25	29	34	39	44
	5	10	14	19	24	29	34	38	43
2.1	5	9	14	19	23	28	33	38	42
2.2	4	9	13	18	22	26	31	35	40
2.3	4	9	13	17	21	26	30	34	39
2.4	4	8	12	16	20	25	29	33	37
2.5	4	8	12	16	20	23	27	31	35
2.6	4	8	11	15	19	23	27	30	34
2.7	4	7	11	15	19	22	26	30	33
	4	7	11	14	18	22	25	29	32
2.8	4	7	11	14	18	21	25	28	32
2.9	3	7	10	14	17	20	24	27	31
3.0	3	7	10	13	16	20	23	26	30
3.1	3	6	10	13	16	19	22	26	29
3.2	3	6	9	12	15	19	22	25	28
3.3	3	6	9	12	15	18	21	24	27
3.4	3	6	9	12	15	17	20	23	26
3.5	3	6	8	11	14	17	20	22	25
3.6	3	5	8	11	14	16	19	22	24
3.7	3	5	8	11	13	16	19	22	24
3.8	3	5	8	10	13	16	18	21	23
3.9	3	5	8	10	13	15	18	20	23
4.0	2	5	7	10	12	15	17	20	22
4.1	2	5	7	10	12	14	17	19	22
4.2	2	5	7	10	12	14	17	19	22
4.3	2	5	7	9	12	14	16	18	21
4.4	2	4	7	9	11	13	15	18	20
4.5	2	4	7	9	11	13	15	18	20
4.6	2	4	7	9	11	13	15	18	20
4.7	2	4	6	8	11	13	15	17	19
4.8	2	4	6	8	10	13	15	17	19
4.9	2	4	6	8	10	12	14	16	18

If $x = y \times 10^{-n}$ with $1 \leqslant y < 10$:

$$\ln x = \ln y + \ln 10^{-n} \approx \ln y - 2.30259\,n$$

For the values of $\ln 10^{-n}$ see the page opposite.

For x near 1, use: $\ln(1 + y) \approx y - \tfrac{1}{2}y^2 + \tfrac{1}{3}y^3$

NATURAL LOGARITHMS ln x or log_e x

$\ln x$ or $\log_e x$

x	0	1	2	3	4	5	6	7	8	9	1 2 3	4 5 6	7 8 9
												ADD	
5.0	1.6094	6114 6134 6154			6174 6194 6214			6233 6253 6273			2 4 6	8 10 12	14 16 18
5.1	1.6292	6312 6332 6351			6371 6390 6409			6429 6448 6467			2 4 6	8 10 12	14 16 18
5.2	1.6487	6506 6525 6544			6563 6582 6601			6620 6639 6658			2 4 6	8 10 11	13 15 17
5.3	1.6677	6696 6715 6734			6752 6771 6790			6808 6827 6845			2 4 6	8 9 11	13 15 17
5.4	1.6864	6882 6901 6919			6938 6956 6974			6993 7011 7029			2 4 5	7 9 11	13 14 16
5.5	1.7047	7066 7084 7102			7120 7138 7156			7174 7192 7210			2 4 5	7 9 11	13 14 16
5.6	1.7228	7246 7263 7281			7299 7317 7334			7352 7370 7387			2 4 5	7 9 11	13 14 16
5.7	1.7405	7422 7440 7457			7475 7492 7509			7527 7544 7561			2 3 5	7 9 10	12 14 15
5.8	1.7579	7596 7613 7630			7647 7664 7681			7699 7716 7733			2 3 5	7 9 10	12 14 15
5.9	1.7750	7766 7783 7800			7817 7834 7851			7867 7884 7901			2 3 5	7 8 10	12 14 15
6.0	1.7918	7934 7951 7967			7984 8001 8017			8034 8050 8066			2 3 5	6 8 10	11 13 14
6.1	1.8083	8099 8116 8132			8148 8165 8181			8197 8213 8229			2 3 5	6 8 10	11 13 14
6.2	1.8245	8262 8278 8294			8310 8326 8342			8358 8374 8390			2 3 5	6 8 10	11 13 14
6.3	1.8405	8421 8437 8453			8469 8485 8500			8516 8532 8547			2 3 5	6 8 10	11 13 14
6.4	1.8563	8579 8594 8610			8625 8641 8656			8672 8687 8703			2 3 5	6 8 10	11 13 14
6.5	1.8718	8733 8749 8764			8779 8795 8810			8825 8840 8856			2 3 5	6 8 9	11 12 14
6.6	1.8871	8886 8901 8916			8931 8946 8961			8976 8991 9006			2 3 5	6 8 9	11 12 14
6.7	1.9021	9036 9051 9066			9081 9095 9110			9125 9140 9155			1 3 4	6 7 9	10 12 13
6.8	1.9169	9184 9199 9213			9228 9242 9257			9272 9286 9301			1 3 4	6 7 9	10 12 13
6.9	1.9315	9330 9344 9359			9373 9387 9402			9416 9430 9445			1 3 4	6 7 8	10 11 13
7.0	1.9459	9473 9488 9502			9516 9530 9544			9559 9573 9587			1 3 4	6 7 8	10 11 13
7.1	1.9601	9615 9629 9643			9657 9671 9685			9699 9713 9727			1 3 4	6 7 8	10 11 13
7.2	1.9741	9755 9769 9782			9796 9810 9824			9838 9851 9865			1 3 4	6 7 8	10 11 13
7.3	1.9879	9892 9906 9920			9933 9947 9961			9974 9988			1 3 4	6 7 8	10 11 13
								2.0001			1 3 4	6 7 8	10 11 13
7.4	2.0015	0028 0042 0055			0069 0082 0096			0109 0122 0136			1 3 4	5 7 8	9 10 12
7.5	2.0149	0162 0176 0189			0202 0215 0229			0242 0255 0268			1 3 4	5 7 8	9 10 12
7.6	2.0281	0295 0308 0321			0334 0347 0360			0373 0386 0399			1 3 4	5 7 8	9 10 12
7.7	2.0412	0425 0438 0451			0464 0477 0490			0503 0516 0528			1 3 4	5 6 8	9 10 12
7.8	2.0541	0554 0567 0580			0592 0605 0618			0631 0643 0656			1 3 4	5 6 8	9 10 12
7.9	2.0669	0681 0694 0707			0719 0732 0744			0757 0769 0782			1 2 4	5 6 7	8 10 11
8.0	2.0794	0807 0819 0832			0844 0857 0869			0882 0894 0906			1 2 4	5 6 7	8 10 11
8.1	2.0919	0931 0943 0956			0968 0980 0992			1005 1017 1029			1 2 4	5 6 7	8 10 11
8.2	2.1041	1054 1066 1078			1090 1102 1114			1126 1138 1150			1 2 4	5 6 7	8 10 11
8.3	2.1163	1175 1187 1199			1211 1223 1235			1247 1258 1270			1 2 4	5 6 7	8 10 11
8.4	2.1282	1294 1306 1318			1330 1342 1353			1365 1377 1389			1 2 4	5 6 7	8 10 11
8.5	2.1401	1412 1424 1436			1448 1459 1471			1483 1494 1506			1 2 4	5 6 7	8 10 11
8.6	2.1518	1529 1541 1552			1564 1576 1587			1599 1610 1622			1 2 4	5 6 7	8 10 11
8.7	2.1633	1645 1656 1668			1679 1691 1702			1713 1725 1736			1 2 4	5 6 7	8 10 11
8.8	2.1748	1759 1770 1782			1793 1804 1815			1827 1838 1849			1 2 3	4 6 7	8 9 10
8.9	2.1861	1872 1883 1894			1905 1917 1928			1939 1950 1961			1 2 3	4 6 7	8 9 10
9.0	2.1972	1983 1994 2006			2017 2028 2039			2050 2061 2072			1 2 3	4 6 7	8 9 10
9.1	2.2083	2094 2105 2116			2127 2138 2148			2159 2170 2181			1 2 3	4 5 7	8 9 10
9.2	2.2192	2203 2214 2225			2235 2246 2257			2268 2279 2289			1 2 3	4 5 7	8 9 10
9.3	2.2300	2311 2322 2332			2343 2354 2364			2375 2386 2396			1 2 3	4 5 7	8 9 10
9.4	2.2407	2418 2428 2439			2450 2460 2471			2481 2492 2502			1 2 3	4 5 7	8 9 10
9.5	2.2513	2523 2534 2544			2555 2565 2576			2586 2597 2607			1 2 3	4 5 6	7 8 9
9.6	2.2618	2628 2638 2649			2659 2670 2680			2690 2701 2711			1 2 3	4 5 6	7 8 9
9.7	2.2721	2732 2742 2752			2762 2773 2783			2793 2803 2814			1 2 3	4 5 6	7 8 9
9.8	2.2824	2834 2844 2854			2865 2875 2885			2895 2905 2915			1 2 3	4 5 6	7 8 9
9.9	2.2925	2935 2946 2956			2966 2976 2986			2996 3006 3016			1 2 3	4 5 6	7 8 9

If $x = y \times 10^n$, with $1 \leqslant y < 10$:

$$\ln x = \ln y + \ln 10^n \approx \ln y + 2.30259\, n$$

n	1	2	3	4	5	6	7	8	9	10
ln 10^n	2.3026	4.6052	6.9078	9.2103	11.5129	13.8155	16.1181	18.4207	20.7233	23.0259
ln 10^{-n}	3.6974	5.3948	7.0922	10.7897	12.4871	14.1845	17.8819	19.5793	21.2767	24.9741

EXPONENTIAL, HYPERBOLIC AND CIRCULAR FUNCTIONS

x	e^x	Δ	e^{-x}	Δ	sinh x	Δ	cosh x	Δ	tanh x	Δ	deg.	sin x	Δ	cos x	Δ	tan x	Δ
rad		+		−		+		+		+	°		+		−		+
0.00	1.000	10	1.0000	100	.0000	100	1.000		.0000	100	0.00	.0000	100	1.0000	0	.0000	100
0.01	1.010	10	0.9900	98	.0100	100	1.000		.0100	100	0.57	.0100	100	1.0000	2	.0100	100
0.02	1.020	10	.9802	98	.0200	100	1.000		.0200	100	1.15	.0200	100	0.9998	2	.0200	100
0.03	1.030	11	.9704	96	.0300	100	1.000	1	.0300	100	1.72	.0300	100	.9996	4	.0300	100
0.04	1.041	10	.9608	96	.0400	100	1.001	0	.0400	100	2.29	.0400	100	.9992	4	.0400	100
0.05	1.051	11	0.9512	94	.0500	100	1.001	1	0500	99	2.86	.0500	100	0.9988	6	.0500	101
0.06	1.062	11	.9418	94	.0600	101	1.002	0	.0599	100	3.44	.0600	99	.9982	6	.0601	101
0.07	1.073	10	.9324	93	.0701	100	1.002	1	.0699	99	4.01	.0699	100	.9976	8	.0701	101
0.08	1.083	11	.9231	92	.0801	100	1.003	1	.0798	100	4.58	.0799	100	.9968	8	.0802	100
0.09	1.094	11	.9139	91	.0901	101	1.004	1	.0898	99	5.16	.0899	99	.9960	10	.0902	101
0.10	1.105	11	0.9048	90	.1002	100	1.005	1	.0997	99	5.73	.0998	100	0.9950	10	.1003	101
0.11	1.116	11	.8958	89	.1102	101	1.006	1	.1096	98	6.30	.1098	99	.9940	12	.1104	102
0.12	1.127	12	.8869	88	.1203	101	1.007	1	.1194	99	6.88	.1197	99	.9928	12	.1206	101
0.13	1.139	11	.8781	87	.1304	101	1.008	2	.1293	98	7.45	.1296	99	.9916	14	.1307	102
0.14	1.150	12	.8694	87	.1405	101	1.010	1	.1391	98	8.02	.1395	99	.9902	14	.1409	102
0.15	1.162	12	0.8607	86	.1506	101	1.011	2	.1489	97	8.59	.1494	99	0.9888	16	.1511	103
0.16	1.174	11	.8521	84	.1607	101	1.013	1	.1586	98	9.17	.1593	99	.9872	16	.1614	103
0.17	1.185	12	.8437	84	.1708	102	1.014	2	.1684	97	9.74	.1692	98	.9856	18	.1717	103
0.18	1.197	12	.8353	83	.1810	101	1.016	2	.1781	96	10.31	.1790	99	.9838	18	.1820	103
0.19	1.209	12	.8270	83	.1911	102	1.018	2	.1877	97	10.89	.1889	98	.9820	19	.1923	104
0.20	1.221	13	0.8187	81	.2013	102	1.020	2	.1974	96	11.46	.1987	98	0.9801	21	.2027	104
0.21	1.234	12	.8106	81	.2115	103	1.022	2	.2070	95	12.03	.2085	97	.9780	21	.2131	105
0.22	1.246	13	.8025	80	.2218	102	1.024	3	.2165	95	12.61	.2182	98	.9759	22	.2236	105
0.23	1.259	12	.7945	79	.2320	103	1.027	2	.2260	95	13.18	.2280	97	.9737	24	.2341	106
0.24	1.271	13	.7866	78	.2423	103	1.029	2	.2355	94	13.75	.2377	97	.9713	24	.2447	106
0.25	1.284	13	0.7788	77	.2526	103	1.031	3	.2449	94	14.32	.2474	97	0.9689	25	.2553	107
0.26	1.297	13	.7711	77	.2629	104	1.034	3	.2543	93	14.90	.2571	96	.9664	26	.2660	108
0.27	1.310	13	.7634	76	.2733	104	1.037	2	.2636	93	15.47	.2667	97	.9638	27	.2768	108
0.28	1.323	13	.7558	75	.2837	104	1.039	3	.2729	92	16.04	.2764	96	.9611	29	.2876	108
0.29	1.336	14	.7483	75	.2941	104	1.042	3	.2821	92	16.62	.2860	95	.9582	29	.2984	109
0.30	1.350	13	0.7408	74	.3045	105	1.045	3	.2913	91	17.19	.2955	96	0.9553	30	.3093	110
0.31	1.363	14	.7334	73	.3150	105	1.048	4	.3004	91	17.76	.3051	95	.9523	31	.3203	111
0.32	1.377	14	.7261	72	.3255	105	1.052	3	.3095	90	18.33	.3146	94	.9492	32	.3314	111
0.33	1.391	14	.7189	71	.3360	106	1.055	3	.3185	90	18.91	.3240	95	.9460	32	.3425	112
0.34	1.405	14	.7118	71	.3466	106	1.058	4	.3275	89	19.48	.3335	94	.9428	34	.3537	113
0.35	1.419	14	0.7047	70	.3572	106	1.062	4	.3364	88	20.05	.3429	94	0.9394	35	.3650	114
0.36	1.433	15	.6977	70	.3678	107	1.066	3	.3452	88	20.63	.3523	93	.9359	36	.3764	115
0.37	1.448	14	.6907	68	.3785	107	1.069	4	.3540	87	21.20	.3616	93	.9323	36	.3879	115
0.38	1.462	15	.6839	68	.3892	108	1.073	4	.3627	87	21.77	.3709	93	.9287	38	.3994	117
0.39	1.477	15	.6771	68	.4000	108	1.077	4	.3714	85	22.35	.3802	92	.9249	38	.4111	117
0.40	1.492	15	0.6703	66	.4108	108	1.081	4	.3799	86	22.92	.3894	92	0.9211	40	.4228	118
0.41	1.507	15	.6637	67	.4216	109	1.085	5	.3885	84	23.49	.3986	92	.9171	40	.4346	120
0.42	1.522	15	.6570	65	.4325	109	1.090	4	.3969	84	24.06	.4078	91	.9131	41	.4466	120
0.43	1.537	16	.6505	65	.4434	109	1.094	4	.4053	83	24.64	.4169	90	.9090	42	.4586	122
0.44	1.553	15	.6440	64	.4543	110	1.098	5	.4136	83	25.21	.4259	91	.9048	44	.4708	123
0.45	1.568	16	0.6376	63	.4653	111	1.103	5	.4219	82	25.78	.4350	89	0.9004	43	.4831	123
0.46	1.584	16	.6313	63	.4764	111	1.108	4	.4301	81	26.36	.4439	90	.8961	45	.4954	126
0.47	1.600	16	.6250	62	.4875	111	1.112	5	.4382	80	26.93	.4529	89	.8916	46	.5080	126
0.48	1.616	16	.6188	62	.4986	112	1.117	5	.4462	80	27.50	.4618	88	.8870	47	.5206	128
0.49	1.632	17	.6126	61	.5098	113	1.122	6	.4542	79	28.07	.4706	88	.8823	47	.5334	129
0.50	1.649	16	0.6065	60	.5211	113	1.128	5	.4621	78	28.65	.4794	88	0.8776	49	.5463	131
0.51	1.665	17	.6005	60	.5324	114	1.133	5	.4699	78	29.22	.4882	87	.8727	49	.5594	132
0.52	1.682	17	.5945	59	.5438	114	1.138	6	.4777	77	29.79	.4969	86	.8678	50	.5726	133
0.53	1.699	17	.5886	59	.5552	114	1.144	5	.4854	76	30.37	.5055	86	.8628	51	.5859	135
0.54	1.716	17	.5827	58	.5666	116	1.149	6	.4930	75	30.94	.5141	86	.8577	52	.5994	137

For interpolation use PPs of the given differences (see p. 45).

EXPONENTIAL, HYPERBOLIC AND CIRCULAR FUNCTIONS

x	e^x	Δ	e^{-x}	Δ	sinh x	Δ	cosh x	Δ	tanh x	Δ	deg.	sin x	Δ	cos x	Δ	tan x	Δ
rad.		+		−		+		+		+	°		+		−		+
0.55	1.733	18	.5769	57	0.578	12	1.155	6	.5005	75	31.51	.5227	85	.8525	52	0.613	14
0.56	1.751	17	.5712	57	.590	11	1.161	6	.5080	74	32.09	.5312	84	.8473	54	.627	14
0.57	1.768	18	.5655	56	.601	12	1.167	6	.5154	73	32.66	.5396	84	.8419	54	.641	14
0.58	1.786	18	.5599	56	.613	12	1.173	6	.5227	72	33.23	.5480	84	.8365	56	.655	15
0.59	1.804	18	.5543	55	.625	12	1.179	6	.5299	71	33.80	.5564	82	.8309	56	.670	14
0.60	1.822	18	.5488	54	0.637	12	1.185	7	.5370	71	34.38	.5646	83	.8253	57	0.684	15
0.61	1.840	19	.5434	55	.649	11	1.192	6	.5441	70	34.95	.5729	81	.8196	57	.699	15
0.62	1.859	19	.5379	53	.660	13	1.198	7	.5511	70	35.52	.5810	81	.8139	59	.714	15
0.63	1.878	18	.5326	53	.673	12	1.205	7	.5581	68	36.10	.5891	81	.8080	59	.729	16
0.64	1.896	20	.5273	53	.685	12	1.212	7	.5649	68	36.67	.5972	80	.8021	60	.745	15
0.65	1.916	19	.5220	51	0.697	12	1.219	7	.5717	67	37.24	.6052	79	.7961	61	0.760	16
0.66	1.935	19	.5169	52	.709	12	1.226	7	.5784	66	37.82	.6131	79	.7900	62	.776	16
0.67	1.954	20	.5117	51	.721	13	1.233	7	.5850	65	38.39	.6210	78	.7838	62	.792	17
0.68	1.974	20	.5066	50	.734	12	1.240	8	.5915	65	38.96	.6288	77	.7776	64	.809	16
0.69	1.994	20	.5016	50	.746	13	1.248	7	.5980	64	39.53	.6365	77	.7712	64	.825	17
0.70	2.014	20	.4966	50	0.759	12	1.255	8	.6044	63	40.11	.6442	76	.7648	64	0.842	18
0.71	2.034	20	.4916	48	.771	13	1.263	8	.6107	62	40.68	.6518	76	.7584	66	.860	17
0.72	2.054	21	.4868	49	.784	13	1.271	7	.6169	62	41.25	.6594	75	.7518	66	.877	18
0.73	2.075	21	.4819	48	.797	12	1.278	9	.6231	60	41.83	.6669	74	.7452	67	.895	18
0.74	2.096	21	.4771	47	.809	13	1.287	8	.6291	60	42.40	.6743	73	.7385	68	.913	19
0.75	2.117	21	.4724	47	0.822	13	1.295	8	.6351	60	42.97	.6816	73	.7317	69	0.932	18
0.76	2.138	22	.4677	47	.835	13	1.303	8	.6411	58	43.54	.6889	72	.7248	69	.950	20
0.77	2.160	21	.4630	46	.848	14	1.311	9	.6469	58	44.12	.6961	72	.7179	70	.970	19
0.78	2.181	22	.4584	46	.862	13	1.320	9	.6527	57	44.69	.7033	71	.7109	71	0.989	20
0.79	2.203	23	.4538	45	.875	13	1.329	8	.6584	56	45.26	.7104	70	.7038	71	1.009	21
0.80	2.226	22	.4493	44	0.888	14	1.337	9	.6640	56	45.84	.7174	69	.6967	72	1.030	20
0.81	2.248	22	.4449	45	.902	13	1.346	9	.6696	55	46.41	.7243	68	.6895	73	1.050	22
0.82	2.270	23	.4404	44	.915	14	1.355	10	.6751	54	46.98	.7311	68	.6822	73	1.072	21
0.83	2.293	23	.4360	43	.929	13	1.365	9	.6805	53	47.56	.7379	67	.6749	74	1.093	23
0.84	2.316	24	.4317	43	.942	14	1.374	10	.6858	53	48.13	.7446	67	.6675	75	1.116	22
0.85	2.340	23	.4274	42	0.956	14	1.384	9	.6911	52	48.70	.7513	65	.6600	76	1.138	24
0.86	2.363	24	.4232	42	.970	14	1.393	10	.6963	51	49.27	.7578	65	.6524	76	1.162	23
0.87	2.387	24	.4190	42	.984	14	1.403	10	.7014	50	49.85	.7643	64	.6448	76	1.185	25
0.88	2.411	24	.4148	41	0.998	14	1.413	10	.7064	50	50.42	.7707	64	.6372	78	1.210	25
0.89	2.435	25	.4107	41	1.012	15	1.423	10	.7114	49	50.99	.7771	62	.6294	78	1.235	25
0.90	2.460	24	.4066	41	1.027	14	1.433	10	.7163	48	51.57	.7833	62	.6216	79	1.260	26
0.91	2.484	25	.4025	40	1.041	14	1.443	11	.7211	48	52.14	.7895	61	.6137	79	1.286	27
0.92	2.509	26	.3985	39	1.055	15	1.454	11	.7259	47	52.71	.7956	60	.6058	80	1.313	28
0.93	2.535	25	.3946	40	1.070	15	1.465	10	.7306	46	53.29	.8016	60	.5978	80	1.341	28
0.94	2.560	26	.3906	39	1.085	14	1.475	11	.7352	46	53.86	.8076	58	.5898	81	1.369	29
0.95	2.586	26	.3867	38	1.099	15	1.486	11	.7398	45	54.43	.8134	58	.5817	82	1.398	30
0.96	2.612	26	.3829	38	1.114	15	1.497	12	.7443	44	55.00	.8192	57	.5735	82	1.428	31
0.97	2.638	26	.3791	38	1.129	16	1.509	11	.7487	44	55.58	.8249	56	.5653	83	1.459	32
0.98	2.664	27	.3753	37	1.145	15	1.520	11	.7531	43	56.15	.8305	55	.5570	83	1.491	33
0.99	2.691	27	.3716	37	1.160	15	1.531	12	.7574	42	56.72	.8360	55	.5487	84	1.524	33
1.00	2.718	28	.3679	37	1.175	16	1.543	12	.7616	42	57.30	.8415	53	.5403	84	1.557	35
1.01	2.746	27	.3642	36	1.191	15	1.555	12	.7658	41	57.87	.8468	53	.5319	85	1.592	36
1.02	2.773	28	.3606	36	1.206	16	1.567	12	.7699	40	58.44	.8521	52	.5234	86	1.628	37
1.03	2.801	28	.3570	35	1.222	16	1.579	12	.7739	40	59.01	.8573	51	.5148	86	1.665	39
1.04	2.829	29	.3535	36	1.238	16	1.591	13	.7779	39	59.59	.8624	50	.5062	86	1.704	39
1.05	2.858	28	.3499	34	1.254	16	1.604	12	.7818	39	60.16	.8674	50	.4976	87	1.743	41
1.06	2.886	29	.3465	35	1.270	16	1.616	13	.7857	38	60.73	.8724	48	.4889	88	1.784	43
1.07	2.915	30	.3430	34	1.286	17	1.629	13	.7895	37	61.31	.8772	48	.4801	88	1.827	44
1.08	2.945	29	.3396	34	1.303	16	1.642	13	.7932	37	61.88	.8820	46	.4713	88	1.871	46
1.09	2.974	30	.3362	33	1.319	17	1.655	14	.7969	36	62.45	.8866	46	.4625	89	1.917	48

Add PPs for Δ+, *subtract* for Δ−. For degrees Δ = +57 or +58.

EXPONENTIAL, HYPERBOLIC AND CIRCULAR FUNCTIONS

x	e^x	Δ	e^{-x}	Δ	sinh x	Δ	cosh x	Δ	tanh x	Δ	deg.	sin x	Δ	cos x	Δ	tan x	Δ
rad		+		−		+		+		+	°		+		−		+
1.10	3.004	30	.3329	33	1.336	16	1.669	13	.8005	36	63.03	.8912	45	.4536	89	1.965	49
1.11	3.034	31	.3296	33	1.352	17	1.682	14	.8041	35	63.60	.8957	44	.4447	90	2.014	52
1.12	3.065	31	.3263	33	1.369	17	1.696	13	.8076	34	64.17	.9001	43	.4357	90	2.066	54
1.13	3.096	31	.3230	32	1.386	17	1.709	14	.8110	34	64.74	.9044	42	.4267	91	2.120	56
1.14	3.127	31	.3198	32	1.403	18	1.723	14	.8144	34	65.32	.9086	42	.4176	91	2.176	58
1.15	3.158	32	.3166	31	1.421	17	1.737	15	.8178	32	65.89	.9128	40	.4085	92	2.234	62
1.16	3.190	32	.3135	31	1.438	18	1.752	14	.8210	33	66.46	.9168	40	.3993	91	2.296	64
1.17	3.222	32	.3104	31	1.456	18	1.766	15	.8243	32	67.04	.9208	38	.3902	93	2.360	67
1.18	3.254	33	.3073	31	1.474	17	1.781	15	.8275	31	67.61	.9246	38	.3809	92	2.427	71
1.19	3.287	33	.3042	30	1.491	18	1.796	15	.8306	31	68.18	.9284	36	.3717	93	2.498	74
1.20	3.320	33	.3012	30	1.509	19	1.811	15	.8337	30	68.75	.9320	36	.3624	94	2.572	78
1.21	3.353	34	.2982	30	1.528	18	1.826	15	.8367	30	69.33	.9356	35	.3530	94	2.650	83
1.22	3.387	34	.2952	29	1.546	18	1.841	16	.8397	29	69.90	.9391	34	.3436	94	2.733	87
1.23	3.421	35	.2923	29	1.564	19	1.857	15	.8426	29	70.47	.9425	33	.3342	94	2.820	92†
1.24	3.456	34	.2894	29	1.583	19	1.872	16	.8455	28	71.05	.9458	32	.3248	95	2.912	98†
1.25	3.490	35	.2865	28	1.602	19	1.888	17	.8483	28	71.62	.9490	31	.3153	95	3.010	103†
1.26	3.525	36	.2837	29	1.621	19	1.905	16	.8511	27	72.19	.9521	30	.3058	95	3.113	111†
1.27	3.561	36	.2808	28	1.640	19	1.921	16	.8538	27	72.77	.9551	29	.2963	96	3.22	12
1.28	3.597	36	.2780	27	1.659	20	1.937	17	.8565	26	73.34	.9580	28	.2867	96	3.34	13
1.29	3.633	36	.2753	28	1.679	19	1.954	17	.8591	26	73.91	.9608	28	.2771	96	3.47	13
1.30	3.669	37	.2725	27	1.698	20	1.971	17	.8617	26	74.48	.9636	26	.2675	96	3.60	15
1.31	3.706	37	.2698	27	1.718	20	1.988	17	.8643	25	75.06	.9662	25	.2579	97	3.75	15
1.32	3.743	38	.2671	26	1.738	20	2.005	18	.8668	24	75.63	.9687	24	.2482	97	3.90	17
1.33	3.781	38	.2645	27	1.758	21	2.023	17	.8692	25	76.20	.9711	24	.2385	97	4.07	19
1.34	3.819	38	.2618	26	1.779	20	2.040	18	.8717	24	76.78	.9735	22	.2288	98	4.26	20
1.35	3.857	39	.2592	25	1.799	21	2.058	18	.8741	23	77.35	.9757	22	.2190	98	4.46	21
1.36	3.896	39	.2567	26	1.820	21	2.076	19	.8764	23	77.92	.9779	20	.2092	98	4.67	24
1.37	3.935	40	.2541	25	1.841	21	2.095	18	.8787	23	78.50	.9799	20	.1994	98	4.91	27
1.38	3.975	40	.2516	25	1.862	21	2.113	19	.8810	22	79.07	.9819	18	.1896	98	5.18	29
1.39	4.015	40	.2491	25	1.883	21	2.132	19	.8832	22	79.64	.9837	17	.1798	98	5.47	33
1.40	4.055	41	.2466	25	1.904	22	2.151	19	.8854	21	80.21	.9854	17	.1700	99	5.80	37
1.41	4.096	41	.2441	24	1.926	22	2.170	19	.8875	21	80.79	.9871	16	.1601	99	6.17	41†
1.42	4.137	42	.2417	24	1.948	22	2.189	20	.8896	21	81.36	.9887	14	.1502	99	6.58	48†
1.43	4.179	42	.2393	24	1.970	22	2.209	20	.8917	20	81.93	.9901	14	.1403	99	7.06	54†
1.44	4.221	42	.2369	23	1.992	22	2.229	20	.8937	20	82.51	.9915	12	.1304	99	7.60	*
1.45	4.263	43	.2346	24	2.014	23	2.249	20	.8957	20	83.08	.9927	12	.1205	99	8.24	
1.46	4.306	43	.2322	23	2.037	23	2.269	21	.8977	19	83.65	.9939	10	.1106	100	8.99	
1.47	4.349	44	.2299	23	2.060	23	2.290	20	.8996	19	84.22	.9949	10	.1006	99	9.89	
1.48	4.393	44	.2276	22	2.083	23	2.310	21	.9015	18	84.80	.9959	8	.0907	100	10.98	
1.49	4.437	45	.2254	23	2.106	23	2.331	21	.9033	18	85.37	.9967	8	.0807	100	12.35	
1.50	4.482	45	.2231	22	2.129	24	2.352	22	.9051	18	85.94	.9975	7	.0707	99	14.1	
1.51	4.527	45	.2209	22	2.153	24	2.374	21	.9069	18	86.52	.9982	5	.0608	100	16.4	
1.52	4.572	46	.2187	22	2.177	24	2.395	22	.9087	17	87.09	.9987	5	.0508	100	19.7	
1.53	4.618	47	.2165	21	2.201	24	2.417	22	.9104	17	87.66	.9992	3	.0408	100	24.5	
1.54	4.665	46	.2144	22	2.225	25	2.439	23	.9121	17	88.24	.9995	3	.0308	100	32.5	
1.55	4.711	48	.2122	21	2.250	24	2.462	22	.9138	16	88.81	.9998	1	.0208	100	48.1	
1.56	4.759	48	.2101	21	2.274	25	2.484	23	.9154	16	89.38	.9999	1	.0108	100	92.6	
1.57	4.807	48	.2080	20	2.299	25	2.507	23	.9170	16	89.95	1.0000		.0008		1256	
1.58	4.855	49	.2060	21	2.324	26	2.530	24	.9186	15							
1.59	4.904	49	.2039	20	2.350	26	2.554	23	.9201	16							
1.60	4.953	50	.2019	20	2.376	25	2.577	24	.9217	15							
1.61	5.003	50	.1999	20	2.401	27	2.601	24	.9232	14							
1.62	5.053	51	.1979	20	2.428	26	2.625	25	.9246	15							
1.63	5.104	51	.1959	19	2.454	27	2.650	25	.9261	14							
1.64	5.155	52	.1940	20	2.481	26	2.675	25	.9275	14							

† The error of linear interpolation may be up to 2 units in the last figure.

* For $x > 1.44$ interpolation by PPs is inaccurate. Convert to degrees, and see p. 19.

x	e^x	Δ	e^{-x}	Δ	$\sinh x$ Δ	$\cosh x$ Δ	$\tanh x$ Δ	x	e^x	Δ	e^{-x}	Δ	$\tanh x$ Δ
		+		−		+		+			+		−		+
1.65	5.207	52	.1920	19	2.507 28	2.700 25	.9289 13	2.20	9.025	91	.1108	11	.9757 5
1.66	5.259	53	.1901	19	2.535 27	2.725 25	.9302 14	2.21	9.116	91	.1097	11	.9762 5
1.67	5.312	54	.1882	18	2.562 28	2.750 26	.9316 13	2.22	9.207	93	.1086	11	.9767 4
1.68	5.366	53	.1864	19	2.590 27	2.776 26	.9329 12	2.23	9.300	93	.1075	10	.9771 5
1.69	5.419	55	.1845	18	2.617 29	2.802 26	.9341 13	2.24	9.393	95	.1065	11	.9776 4
1.70	5.474	55	.1827	18	2.646 28	2.828 27	.9354 12	2.25	9.488	95	.1054	10	.9780 5
1.71	5.529	56	.1809	18	2.674 29	2.855 27	.9366 13	2.26	9.583	96	.1044	11	.9785 4
1.72	5.585	56	.1791	18	2.703 29	2.882 27	.9379 12	2.27	9.679	98	.1033	10	.9789 4
1.73	5.641	56	.1773	18	2.732 29	2.909 27	.9391 11	2.28	9.777	98	.1023	10	.9793 4
1.74	5.697	58	.1755	17	2.761 29	2.936 28	.9402 12	2.29	9.875	99	.1013	10	.9797 4
1.75	5.755	57	.1738	18	2.790 30	2.964 28	.9414 11	2.30	9.974	100	.1003	10	.9801 4
1.76	5.812	59	.1720	17	2.820 30	2.992 29	.9425 11	2.31	10.07	11	.09926	99	.9805 4
1.77	5.871	59	.1703	17	2.850 31	3.021 28	.9436 11	2.32	10.18	10	.09827	97	.9809 4
1.78	5.930	59	.1686	16	2.881 30	3.049 29	.9447 11	2.33	10.28	10	.09730	97	.9812 4
1.79	5.989	61	.1670	17	2.911 31	3.078 29	.9458 10	2.34	10.38	11	.09633	96	.9816 4
1.80	6.050	60	.1653	16	2.942 31	3.107 30	.9468 10	2.35	10.49	10	.09537	95	.9820 3
1.81	6.110	62	.1637	17	2.973 32	3.137 30	.9478 10	2.36	10.59	11	.09442	94	.9823 4
1.82	6.172	62	.1620	16	3.005 32	3.167 30	.9488 10	2.37	10.70	10	.09348	93	.9827 3
1.83	6.234	63	.1604	16	3.037 32	3.197 31	.9498 10	2.38	10.80	11	.09255	92	.9830 3
1.84	6.297	63	.1588	16	3.069 32	3.228 31	.9508 9	2.39	10.91	11	.09163	91	.9833 4
1.85	6.360	64	.1572	15	3.101 33	3.259 31	.9517 10	2.40	11.02	11	.09072	90	.9837 3
1.86	6.424	64	.1557	16	3.134 33	3.290 31	.9527 9	2.41	11.13	12	.08982	90	.9840 3
1.87	6.488	66	.1541	15	3.167 33	3.321 32	.9536 9	2.42	11.25	11	.08892	88	.9843 3
1.88	6.554	65	.1526	15	3.200 34	3.353 32	.9545 9	2.43	11.36	11	.08804	88	.9846 3
1.89	6.619	67	.1511	15	3.234 34	3.385 33	.9554 8	2.44	11.47	12	.08716	87	.9849 3
1.90	6.686	67	.1496	15	3.268 35	3.418 33	.9562 9	2.45	11.59	11	.08629	86	.9852 3
1.91	6.753	68	.1481	15	3.303 34	3.451 33	.9571 8	2.46	11.70	12	.08543	85	.9855 3
1.92	6.821	69	.1466	15	3.337 35	3.484 33	.9579 8	2.47	11.82	12	.08458	84	.9858 3
1.93	6.890	69	.1451	14	3.372 36	3.517 34	.9587 8	2.48	11.94	12	.08374	83	.9861 2
1.94	6.959	70	.1437	14	3.408 35	3.551 34	.9595 8	2.49	12.06	12	.08291	83	.9863 3
1.95	7.029	70	.1423	14	3.443 36	3.585 35	.9603 8	2.50	12.18	12	.08208	81	.9866 3
1.96	7.099	72	.1409	14	3.479 37	3.620 35	.9611 7	2.51	12.30	13	.08127	81	.9869 2
1.97	7.171	72	.1395	14	3.516 36	3.655 35	.9618 8	2.52	12.43	12	.08046	80	.9871 3
1.98	7.243	73	.1381	14	3.552 37	3.690 36	.9626 7	2.53	12.55	13	.07966	79	.9874 2
1.99	7.316	73	.1367	14	3.589 38	3.726 36	.9633 7	2.54	12.68	13	.07887	79	.9876 3
2.00	7.389	74	.1353	13	3.627 38	3.762 37	.9640 7	2.55	12.81	13	.07808	78	.9879 2
2.01	7.463	75	.1340	13	3.665 38	3.799 36	.9647 7	2.56	12.94	13	.07730	76	.9881 3
2.02	7.538	76	.1327	14	3.703 38	3.835 38	.9654 7	2.57	13.07	13	.07654	77	.9884 2
2.03	7.614	77	.1313	13	3.741 39	3.873 37	.9661 6	2.58	13.20	13	.07577	75	.9886 2
2.04	7.691	77	.1300	13	3.780 40	3.910 38	.9667 7	2.59	13.33	13	.07502	75	.9888 2
2.05	7.768	78	.1287	12	3.820 39	3.948 39	.9674 6	2.60	13.46	14	.07427	74	.9890 2
2.06	7.846	79	.1275	13	3.859 40	3.987 39	.9680 7	2.61	13.60	14	.07353	73	.9892 3
2.07	7.925	79	.1262	13	3.899 41	4.026 39	.9687 6	2.62	13.74	13	.07280	72	.9895 2
2.08	8.004	81	.1249	12	3.940 41	4.065 39	.9693 6	2.63	13.87	14	.07208	72	.9897 2
2.09	8.085	81	.1237	12	3.981 41	4.104 40	.9699 6	2.64	14.01	14	.07136	71	.9899 2
2.10	8.166	82	.1225	13	4.022 42	4.144 41	.9705 5	2.65	14.15	15	.07065	70	.9901 2
2.11	8.248	83	.1212	12	4.064 42	4.185 41	.9710 6	2.66	14.30	14	.06995	70	.9903 2
2.12	8.331	84	.1200	12	4.106 42	4.226 41	.9716 5	2.67	14.44	15	.06925	69	.9905 1
2.13	8.415	84	.1188	11	4.148 43	4.267 42	.9721 6	2.68	14.59	14	.06856	68	.9906 2
2.14	8.499	86	.1177	12	4.191 43	4.309 42	.9727 5	2.69	14.73	15	.06788	67	.9908 2
2.15	8.585	86	.1165	12	4.234 44	4.351 42	.9732 5	2.70	14.88	15	.06721	67	.9910 2
2.16	8.671	87	.1153	11	4.278 44	4.393 43	.9737 6	2.71	15.03	15	.06654	67	.9912 2
2.17	8.758	88	.1142	12	4.322 45	4.436 44	.9743 5	2.72	15.18	15	.06587	65	.9914 1
2.18	8.846	89	.1130	11	4.367 45	4.480 44	.9748 5	2.73	15.33	16	.06522	65	.9915 2
2.19	8.935	90	.1119	11	4.412 45	4.524 44	.9753 4	2.74	15.49	15	.06457	64	.9917 2

For $x \geqslant 2.2$ use:

$$\sinh x = \tfrac{1}{2}(e^x - e^{-x}) \qquad \cosh x = \tfrac{1}{2}(e^x + e^{-x})$$

[37]

EXPONENTIAL FUNCTIONS

x	e^x	Δ	e^{-x}	Δ	x	e^x	Δ	e^{-x}	Δ	x	e^x	Δ	e^{-x}	Δ	x	e^{-x}	Δ
		+		−			+		−			+		−			−
															4.4	.01228	117
2.75	15.64	16	.06393	64	3.30	27.11	28	.03688	36	3.85	46.99	48	.02128	21	4.5	.01111	106
2.76	15.80	16	.06329	63	3.31	27.39	27	.03652	37	3.86	47.47	47	.02107	21	4.6	.01005	95
2.77	15.96	16	.06266	62	3.32	27.66	28	.03615	36	3.87	47.94	48	.02086	21	4.7	.00910	87
2.78	16.12	16	.06204	62	3.33	27.94	28	.03579	35	3.88	48.42	49	.02065	20	4.8	.00823	78
2.79	16.28	16	.06142	61	3.34	28.22	28	.03544	36	3.89	48.91	49	.02045	21	4.9	.00745	71
2.80	16.44	17	.06081	61	3.35	28.50	29	.03508	34	3.90	49.40	50	.02024	20	5.0	.00674	64
2.81	16.61	17	.06020	59	3.36	28.79	29	.03474	35	3.91	49.90	50	.02004	20	5.1	.00610	58
2.82	16.78	17	.05961	60	3.37	29.08	29	.03439	34	3.92	50.40	51	.01984	20	5.2	.00552	53
2.83	16.95	17	.05901	58	3.38	29.37	30	.03405	34	3.93	50.91	51	.01964	19	5.3	.00499	47
2.84	17.12	17	.05843	59	3.39	29.67	29	.03371	34	3.94	51.42	52	.01945	20	5.4	.00452	43
2.85	17.29	17	.05784	57	3.40	29.96	31	.03337	33	3.95	51.94	52	.01925	19	5.5	.00409	39
2.86	17.46	18	.05727	57	3.41	30.27	30	.03304	33	3.96	52.46	52	.01906	19	5.6	.00370	35
2.87	17.64	17	.05670	57	3.42	30.57	31	.03271	32	3.97	52.98	54	.01887	18	5.7	.00335	32
2.88	17.81	18	.05613	55	3.43	30.88	31	.03239	33	3.98	53.52	53	.01869	19	5.8	.00303	29
2.89	17.99	18	.05558	56	3.44	31.19	31	.03206	31	3.99	54.05	55	.01850	18	5.9	.00274	26
2.90	18.17	19	.05502	54	3.45	31.50	32	.03175	32	4.00	54.60	55	.01832	19	6.0	.00248	24
2.91	18.36	18	.05448	55	3.46	31.82	32	.03143	31	4.01	55.15	55	.01813	18	6.1	.00224	21
2.92	18.54	19	.05393	53	3.47	32.14	32	.03112	31	4.02	55.70	56	.01795	18	6.2	.00203	19
2.93	18.73	19	.05340	53	3.48	32.46	33	.03081	31	4.03	56.26	57	.01777	17	6.3	.00184	18
2.94	18.92	19	.05287	53	3.49	32.79	33	.03050	30	4.04	56.83	57	.01760	18	6.4	.00166	16
2.95	19.11	19	.05234	52	3.50	33.12	33	.03020	30	4.05	57.40	57	.01742	17	6.5	.00150	14
2.96	19.30	19	.05182	52	3.51	33.45	33	.02990	30	4.06	57.97	59	.01725	17	6.6	.00136	13
2.97	19.49	20	.05130	51	3.52	33.78	34	.02960	30	4.07	58.56	59	.01708	17	6.7	.00123	12
2.98	19.69	20	.05079	50	3.53	34.12	35	.02930	29	4.08	59.15	59	.01691	17	6.8	.00111	10
2.99	19.89	20	.05029	50	3.54	34.47	34	.02901	29	4.09	59.74	60	.01674	17	6.9	.00101	10
3.00	20.09	20	.04979	50	3.55	34.81	35	.02872	28	4.10	60.34	61	.01657	16	7.0	$.0^3912$	87
3.01	20.29	20	.04929	49	3.56	35.16	36	.02844	28	4.11	60.95	61	.01641	17	7.1	$.0^3825$	78
3.02	20.49	21	.04880	48	3.57	35.52	35	.02816	28	4.12	61.56	62	.01624	16	7.2	$.0^3747$	71
3.03	20.70	21	.04832	49	3.58	35.87	36	.02788	28	4.13	62.18	62	.01608	16	7.3	$.0^3676$	65
3.04	20.91	21	.04783	47	3.59	36.23	37	.02760	28	4.14	62.80	63	.01592	16	7.4	$.0^3611$	58
3.05	21.12	21	.04736	47	3.60	36.60	37	.02732	27	4.15	63.43	64	.01576	15	7.5	$.0^3553$	53
3.06	21.33	21	.04689	47	3.61	36.97	37	.02705	27	4.16	64.07	65	.01561	16	7.6	$.0^3500$	47
3.07	21.54	22	.04642	46	3.62	37.34	37	.02678	26	4.17	64.72	65	.01545	15	7.7	$.0^3453$	43
3.08	21.76	22	.04596	46	3.63	37.71	38	.02652	27	4.18	65.37	65	.01530	15	7.8	$.0^3410$	39
3.09	21.98	22	.04550	45	3.64	38.09	38	.02625	26	4.19	66.02	67	.01515	15	7.9	$.0^3371$	36
3.10	22.20	22	.04505	45	3.65	38.47	39	.02599	26	4.20	66.69	67	.01500	15	8.0	$.0^3335$	31
3.11	22.42	23	.04460	44	3.66	38.86	39	.02573	25	4.21	67.36	67	.01485	15	8.1	$.0^3304$	29
3.12	22.65	22	.04416	44	3.67	39.25	40	.02548	26	4.22	68.03	69	.01470	15	8.2	$.0^3275$	26
3.13	22.87	23	.04372	44	3.68	39.65	39	.02522	25	4.23	68.72	69	.01455	14	8.3	$.0^3249$	24
3.14	23.10	24	.04328	43	3.69	40.04	41	.02497	25	4.24	69.41	70	.01441	15	8.4	$.0^3225$	22
3.15	23.34	23	.04285	42	3.70	40.45	40	.02472	24	4.25	70.11	70	.01426	14	8.5	$.0^3203$	19
3.16	23.57	24	.04243	43	3.71	40.85	41	.02448	25	4.26	70.81	71	.01412	14	8.6	$.0^3184$	17
3.17	23.81	24	.04200	41	3.72	41.26	42	.02423	24	4.27	71.52	72	.01398	14	8.7	$.0^3167$	16
3.18	24.05	24	.04159	42	3.73	41.68	42	.02399	24	4.28	72.24	73	.01384	14	8.8	$.0^3151$	15
3.19	24.29	24	.04117	41	3.74	42.10	42	.02375	23	4.29	72.97	73	.01370	13	8.9	$.0^3136$	13
3.20	24.53	25	.04076	40	3.75	42.52	43	.02352	24	4.30	73.70	74	.01357	14	9.0	$.0^3123$	11
3.21	24.78	25	.04036	40	3.76	42.95	43	.02328	23	4.31	74.44	75	.01343	13	9.1	$.0^3112$	11
3.22	25.03	25	.03996	40	3.77	43.38	44	.02305	23	4.32	75.19	75	.01330	13	9.2	$.0^3101$	10
3.23	25.28	25	.03956	40	3.78	43.82	44	.02282	22	4.33	75.94	77	.01317	13	9.3	$.0^4914$	87
3.24	25.53	26	.03916	39	3.79	44.26	44	.02260	23	4.34	76.71	77	.01304	13	9.4	$.0^4827$	78
3.25	25.79	26	.03877	38	3.80	44.70	45	.02237	22	4.35	77.48	78	.01291	13	9.5	$.0^4749$	72
3.26	26.05	26	.03839	38	3.81	45.15	45	.02215	22	4.36	78.26	78	.01278	13	9.6	$.0^4677$	64
3.27	26.31	27	.03801	38	3.82	45.60	46	.02193	22	4.37	79.04	80	.01265	12	9.7	$.0^4613$	58
3.28	26.58	26	.03763	38	3.83	46.06	47	.02171	22	4.38	79.84	80	.01253	13	9.8	$.0^4555$	53
3.29	26.84	27	.03725	37	3.84	46.53	46	.02149	21	4.39	80.64	81	.01240	12	9.9	$.0^4502$	48

For larger values of x use:

$$e^x = 1/e^{-x}$$

$$e^x = \text{antilog } (x \lg e) \qquad e^{-x} = \text{antilog } (-x \lg e) \qquad \lg e \approx 0.43429$$

BINOMIAL COEFFICIENTS $\binom{n}{r}$ or ^nC_r

$$\binom{n}{r} = \binom{n}{n-r}$$

n	0	1	2	3	4	5	6	7	8	9	10
1	1	1									
2	1	2	1								
3	1	3	3	1							
4	1	4	6	4	1						
5	1	5	10	10	5	1					
6	1	6	15	20	15	6	1				
7	1	7	21	35	35	21	7	1			
8	1	8	28	56	70	56	28	8	1		
9	1	9	36	84	126	126	84	36	9	1	
10	1	10	45	120	210	252	210	120	45	10	1
11	1	11	55	165	330	462	462	330	165	55	11
12	1	12	66	220	495	792	924	792	495	220	66
13	1	13	78	286	715	1287	1716	1716	1287	715	286
14	1	14	91	364	1001	2002	3003	3432	3003	2002	1001
15	1	15	105	455	1365	3003	5005	6435	6435	5005	3003
16	1	16	120	560	1820	4368	8008	11440	12870	11440	8008
17	1	17	136	680	2380	6188	12376	19448	24310	24310	19448
18	1	18	153	816	3060	8568	18564	31824	43758	48620	43758
19	1	19	171	969	3876	11628	27132	50388	75582	92378	92378
20	1	20	190	1140	4845	15504	38760	77520	125970	167960	184756

LOWER QUANTILES $r_{[P]}$ OF THE BINOMIAL DISTRIBUTION $B(n, \tfrac{1}{2})$

n	.005	.01	.025	.05	.25	n	.005	.01	.025	.05	.25	n	.005	.01	.025	.05	.25
5	0	0	0	1	2	25	6	7	8	8	11	45	14	15	16	17	20
6	0	0	1	1	2	26	7	7	8	9	11	46	14	15	16	17	21
7	0	1	1	1	3	27	7	8	8	9	12	47	15	16	17	18	21
8	1	1	1	2	3	28	7	8	9	10	12	48	15	16	17	18	22
9	1	1	2	2	3	29	8	8	9	10	13	49	16	16	18	19	22
10	1	1	2	2	4	30	8	9	10	11	13	50	16	17	18	19	23
11	1	2	2	3	4	31	8	9	10	11	14	52	17	18	19	20	24
12	2	2	3	3	5	32	9	9	10	11	14	54	18	19	20	21	25
13	2	2	3	4	5	33	9	10	11	12	15	56	18	19	21	22	25
14	2	3	3	4	6	34	10	10	11	12	15	58	19	20	22	23	26
15	3	3	4	4	6	35	10	11	12	13	16	60	20	21	22	24	27
16	3	3	4	5	7	36	10	11	12	13	16	70	24	25	27	28	32
17	3	4	5	5	7	37	11	11	13	14	16	80	29	30	31	33	37
18	4	4	5	6	8	38	11	12	13	14	17	90	33	34	36	37	42
19	4	5	5	6	8	39	12	12	13	14	17	100	37	38	40	42	47
20	4	5	6	6	8	40	12	13	14	15	18	110	42	43	45	46	51
21	5	5	6	7	9	41	12	13	14	15	18	120	46	47	49	51	56
22	5	6	6	7	9	42	13	14	15	16	19	130	50	52	54	58	61
23	5	6	7	8	10	43	13	14	15	16	19	140	55	56	58	60	66
24	6	6	7	8	10	44	14	14	16	17	20	150	59	61	63	65	71

If the probability of success in a single trial is $\tfrac{1}{2}$ (success and failure being equally probable) the probability of exactly r successes in a sequence of n independent trials is:

$$\binom{n}{r} \times \frac{1}{2^n}$$

This table gives, for P = .005, .01, .025, .05 and .25 (i.e. 0.5%, 1%, 2.5%, 5% and 25%), the smallest number $r_{[P]}$ for which the probability of $r_{[P]}$ successes or fewer is at least P. If $r < r_{[P]}$ the probability of r successes or fewer is less than P. Interpolation n-wise is permissible; the error is at most 1.

[39]

UPPER TAIL PROBABILITIES $Q(z)$ OF THE NORMAL DISTRIBUTION N(0,1)

z	0	1	2	3	4	5	6	7	8	9	1 2 3	4 5 6	7 8 9
												SUBTRACT	
0.0	.5000	.4960	.4920	.4880	.4840	.4801	.4761	.4721	.4681	.4641	4 8 12	16 20 24	28 32 36
0.1	.4602	.4562	.4522	.4483	.4443	.4404	.4364	.4325	.4286	.4247	4 8 12	16 20 24	28 32 36
0.2	.4207	.4168	.4129	.4090	.4052	.4013	.3974	.3936	.3897	.3859	4 8 12	15 19 23	27 31 35
0.3	.3821	.3783	.3745	.3707	.3669	.3632	.3594	.3557	.3520	.3483	4 7 11	15 19 22	26 30 34
0.4	.3446	.3409	.3372	.3336	.3300	.3264	.3228	.3192	.3156	.3121	4 7 11	14 18 22	25 29 32
0.5	.3085	.3050	.3015	.2981	.2946	.2912	.2877	.2843	.2810	.2776	3 7 10	14 17 20	24 27 31
0.6	.2743	.2709	.2676	.2643	.2611	.2578	.2546	.2514	.2483	.2451	3 7 10	13 16 19	23 26 29
0.7	.2420	.2389	.2358	.2327	.2296	.2266	.2236	.2206	.2177	.2148	3 6 9	12 15 18	21 24 27
0.8	.2119	.2090	.2061	.2033	.2005	.1977	.1949	.1922	.1894	.1867	3 5 8	11 14 16	19 22 25
0.9	.1841	.1814	.1788	.1762	.1736	.1711	.1685	.1660	.1635	.1611	3 5 8	10 13 15	18 20 23
1.0	.1587	.1562	.1539	.1515	.1492	.1469	.1446	.1423	.1401	.1379	2 5 7	9 12 14	16 19 21
1.1	.1357	.1335	.1314	.1292	.1271	.1251	.1230	.1210	.1190	.1170	2 4 6	8 10 12	14 16 18
1.2	.1151	.1131	.1112	.1093	.1075	.1056	.1038	.1020	.1003	.0985	2 4 6	7 9 11	13 15 17
1.3	.0968	.0951	.0934	.0918	.0901	.0885	.0869	.0853	.0838	.0823	2 3 5	6 8 10	11 13 14
1.4	.0808	.0793	.0778	.0764	.0749	.0735	.0721	.0708	.0694	.0681	1 3 4	6 7 8	10 11 13
1.5	.0668	.0655	.0643	.0630	.0618	.0606	.0594	.0582	.0571	.0559	1 2 4	5 6 7	8 10 11
1.6	.0548	.0537	.0526	.0516	.0505	.0495	.0485	.0475	.0465	.0455	1 2 3	4 5 6	7 8 9
1.7	.0446	.0436	.0427	.0418	.0409	.0401	.0392	.0384	.0375	.0367	1 2 3	4 4 5	6 7 8
1.8	.0359	.0351	.0344	.0336	.0329	.0322	.0314	.0307	.0301	.0294	1 1 2	3 4 4	5 6 6
1.9	.0287	.0281	.0274	.0268	.0262	.0256	.0250	.0244	.0239	.0233	1 1 2	2 3 4	4 5 5
2.0	.0228	.0222	.0217	.0212	.0207	.0202	.0197	.0192	.0188	.0183	0 1 1	2 2 3	3 4 4
2.1	.0179	.0174	.0170	.0166	.0162	.0158	.0154	.0150	.0146	.0143	0 1 1	2 2 2	3 3 4
2.2	.0139	.0136	.0132	.0129	.0125	.0122	.0119	.0116	.0113	.0110	0 1 1	1 2 2	2 3 3
2.3	.0107	.0104	.0102										
				$.0^2990$	$.0^2964$	$.0^2939$	$.0^2914$				3 5 8	10 13 15	18 20 23
								$.0^2889$	$.0^2866$	$.0^2842$	2 5 7	9 12 14	16 18 21
2.4	$.0^2820$	$.0^2798$	$.0^2776$	$.0^2755$	$.0^2734$						2 4 6	8 11 13	15 17 19
						$.0^2714$	$.0^2695$	$.0^2676$	$.0^2657$	$.0^2639$	2 4 6	7 9 11	13 15 17
2.5	$.0^2621$	$.0^2604$	$.0^2587$	$.0^2570$	$.0^2554$	$.0^2539$	$.0^2523$	$.0^2508$	$.0^2494$	$.0^2480$	2 3 5	6 8 9	11 12 14
2.6	$.0^2466$	$.0^2453$	$.0^2440$	$.0^2427$	$.0^2415$	$.0^2402$	$.0^2391$	$.0^2379$	$.0^2368$	$.0^2357$	1 2 3	5 6 7	8 9 10
2.7	$.0^2347$	$.0^2336$	$.0^2326$	$.0^2317$	$.0^2307$	$.0^2298$	$.0^2289$	$.0^2280$	$.0^2272$	$.0^2264$	1 2 3	4 5 6	7 8 9
2.8	$.0^2256$	$.0^2248$	$.0^2240$	$.0^2233$	$.0^2226$	$.0^2219$	$.0^2212$	$.0^2205$	$.0^2199$	$.0^2193$	1 1 2	3 4 4	5 6 6
2.9	$.0^2187$	$.0^2181$	$.0^2175$	$.0^2169$	$.0^2164$	$.0^2159$	$.0^2154$	$.0^2149$	$.0^2144$	$.0^2139$	0 1 1	2 2 3	3 4 4
3.0	$.0^2135$	$.0^2131$	$.0^2126$	$.0^2122$	$.0^2118$	$.0^2114$	$.0^2111$	$.0^2107$	$.0^2104$	$.0^2100$	0 1 1	2 2 2	3 3 4
3.1	$.0^3968$	$.0^3935$	$.0^3904$								3 6 9	13 16 19	22 25 28
				$.0^3874$	$.0^3845$	$.0^3816$	$.0^3789$				3 6 8	11 14 17	20 22 25
								$.0^3762$	$.0^3736$	$.0^3711$	2 5 7	10 12 15	17 20 22
3.2	$.0^3687$	$.0^3664$	$.0^3641$	$.0^3619$	$.0^3598$						2 4 7	9 11 13	15 18 20
						$.0^3577$	$.0^3557$	$.0^3538$	$.0^3519$	$.0^3501$	2 4 6	8 9 11	13 15 17
3.3	$.0^3483$	$.0^3466$	$.0^3450$	$.0^3434$	$.0^3419$						2 3 5	6 8 10	11 13 14
						$.0^3404$	$.0^3390$	$.0^3376$	$.0^3362$	$.0^3349$	1 3 4	5 7 8	9 10 12
3.4	$.0^3337$	$.0^3325$	$.0^3313$	$.0^3302$	$.0^3291$	$.0^3280$	$.0^3270$	$.0^3260$	$.0^3251$	$.0^3242$	1 2 3	4 5 6	7 8 9
3.5	$.0^3233$	$.0^3224$	$.0^3216$	$.0^3208$	$.0^3200$	$.0^3193$	$.0^3185$	$.0^3178$	$.0^3172$	$.0^3165$	1 1 2	3 4 4	5 6 7
3.6	$.0^3159$	$.0^3153$	$.0^3147$	$.0^3142$	$.0^3136$	$.0^3131$	$.0^3126$	$.0^3121$	$.0^3117$	$.0^3112$	0 1 1	2 2 3	3 4 5
3.7	$.0^3108$	$.0^3104$	$.0^3100$	$.0^496$	$.0^492$	$.0^488$	$.0^485$	$.0^482$	$.0^478$	$.0^475$			
3.8	$.0^472$	$.0^469$	$.0^467$	$.0^464$	$.0^462$	$.0^459$	$.0^457$	$.0^454$	$.0^452$	$.0^450$			
3.9	$.0^448$	$.0^446$	$.0^444$	$.0^442$	$.0^441$	$.0^439$	$.0^437$	$.0^436$	$.0^434$	$.0^433$			

For negative z use the relation:

$$Q(z) = 1 - Q(-z) = P(-z)$$

Example: if $u \sim$ N (0,1), *find* (a) Prob $(u > 2)$, (b) Prob $(0 < u < 2)$, (c) Prob $(|u| > 2)$, (d) Prob $(|u| < 2)$. The desired probabilities are (a) $Q(2) = .0228$, (b) $Q(0) - Q(2) = .5000 - .0228 = .4772$, (c) $2Q(2) = .0456$, (d) $1 - 2Q(2) = .9544$.

If $v \sim$ N(μ, σ^2), Prob $(v > x)$ is given by $Q(z)$ with $z = (x - \mu)/\sigma$.

UPPER QUANTILES $z_{[P]}$ OF THE NORMAL DISTRIBUTION N(0,1)

P	Q	z	P	Q	z	P	Q	z	P	Q	z	Q	z
.50	.50	0.000	.85	.15	1.036	.975	.025	1.960	.990	.010	2.326	$.0^3 4$	3.353
.55	.45	0.126	.86	.14	1.080	.976	.024	1.977	.991	.009	2.366	$.0^3 3$	3.432
.60	.40	0.253	.87	.13	1.126	.977	.023	1.995	.992	.008	2.409	$.0^3 2$	3.540
.65	.35	0.385	.88	.12	1.175	.978	.022	2.014	.993	.007	2.457	$.0^3 1$	3.719
.70	.30	0.524	.89	.11	1.227	.979	.021	2.034	.994	.006	2.512	$.0^4 5$	3.891
.75	.25	0.674	.90	.10	1.282	.980	.020	2.054	.995	.005	2.576	$.0^4 1$	4.265
.76	.24	0.706	.91	.09	1.341	.981	.019	2.075	.996	.004	2.652	$.0^5 5$	4.417
.77	.23	0.739	.92	.08	1.405	.982	.018	2.097	.997	.003	2.748	$.0^5 1$	4.753
.78	.22	0.772	.93	.07	1.476	.983	.017	2.120	.998	.002	2.878	$.0^6 5$	4.892
.79	.21	0.806	.94	.06	1.555	.984	.016	2.144	.999	.001	3.090	$.0^6 1$	5.199
.80	.20	0.842	.950	.050	1.645	.985	.015	2.170	.9991	$.0^3 9$	3.121	$.0^7 5$	5.327
.81	.19	0.878	.955	.045	1.695	.986	.014	2.197	.9992	$.0^3 8$	3.156	$.0^7 1$	5.612
.82	.18	0.915	.960	.040	1.751	.987	.013	2.226	.9993	$.0^3 7$	3.195	$.0^8 5$	5.731
.83	.17	0.954	.965	.035	1.812	.988	.012	2.257	.9994	$.0^3 6$	3.239	$.0^8 1$	5.998
.84	.16	0.994	.970	.030	1.881	.989	.011	2.290	.9995	$.0^3 5$	3.291	$.0^9 5$	6.109

The tabulated function is $z_{[P]}$: if $u \sim \text{N}(0,1)$, Prob $(u < z_{[P]}) = P$, Prob $(u > z_{[P]}) = 1 - P = Q$, and (for $P > \frac{1}{2}$) Prob $(|u| > z_{[P]}) = 2Q$.

Lower quantiles $(P < \frac{1}{2})$ are given by:

$$z_{[P]} = -z_{[1-P]}$$

PROBABILITY DENSITY $\varphi(z)$ OF THE NORMAL DISTRIBUTION N(0,1)

z	0	1	2	3	4	5	6	7	8	9
0.	0.399	.397	.391	.381	.368	.352	.333	.312	.290	.266
1.	0.242	.218	.194	.171	.150	.130	.111	.094	.079	.066
2.	0.0540	.0440	.0355	.0283	.0224	.0175	.0136	.0104	.0079	.0060
3.	0.00443	.00327	.00238	.00172	.00123	.00087	.00061	.00042	.00029	.00020
4.	$0.0^3 134$	$.0^4 89$	$.0^4 59$	$.0^4 39$	$.0^4 25$	$.0^4 16$	$.0^4 10$	$.0^5 64$	$.0^5 40$	$.0^5 24$

For $z < 0$ use the relation:

$$\varphi(z) = \varphi(-z)$$

The tabulated functions are defined thus:

$$\varphi(z) = \sqrt{\left(\frac{1}{2\pi}\right)} \exp\left(-\tfrac{1}{2}z^2\right)$$

$$Q(z) = \int_z^\infty \varphi(u)\,du$$

$$\int_{-\infty}^{z_{[P]}} \varphi(u)\,du = P$$

In the figure the probability density is represented by the ordinate of the graph, and the tail probabilities are represented by areas under the graph.

The probability density of the distribution N(μ, σ^2) is

$$f(x) = \frac{1}{\sigma}\varphi(z)$$

with $z = (x - \mu)/\sigma$.

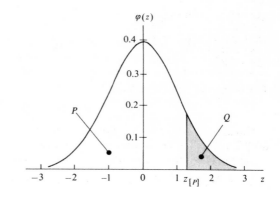

P	.75	.90	.95	.975	.99	.995	.9975	.999	.9995	120
Q	.25	.10	.05	.025	.01	.005	.0025	.001	.0005	v
$2Q$	.50	.20	.10	.050	.02	.010	.0050	.002	.0010	
$v=1$	1.000	3.078	6.314	12.71	31.82	63.66	127.3	318.3	636.6	
2	0.816	1.886	2.920	4.303	6.965	9.925	14.09	22.33	31.60	
3	0.765	1.638	2.353	3.182	4.541	5.841	7.453	10.21	12.92	
4	0.741	1.533	2.132	2.776	3.747	4.604	5.598	7.173	8.610	
5	0.727	1.476	2.015	2.571	3.365	4.032	4.773	5.893	6.869	
6	0.718	1.440	1.943	2.447	3.143	3.707	4.317	5.208	5.959	
7	0.711	1.415	1.895	2.365	2.998	3.499	4.029	4.785	5.408	
8	0.706	1.397	1.860	2.306	2.896	3.355	3.833	4.501	5.041	
9	0.703	1.383	1.833	2.262	2.821	3.250	3.690	4.297	4.781	
10	0.700	1.372	1.812	2.228	2.764	3.169	3.581	4.144	4.587	
11	0.697	1.363	1.796	2.201	2.718	3.106	3.497	4.025	4.437	
12	0.695	1.356	1.782	2.179	2.681	3.055	3.428	3.930	4.318	
13	0.694	1.350	1.771	2.160	2.650	3.012	3.372	3.852	4.221	
14	0.692	1.345	1.761	2.145	2.624	2.977	3.326	3.787	4.140	
15	0.691	1.341	1.753	2.131	2.602	2.947	3.286	3.733	4.073	
16	0.690	1.337	1.746	2.120	2.583	2.921	3.252	3.686	4.015	
17	0.689	1.333	1.740	2.110	2.567	2.898	3.222	3.646	3.965	
18	0.688	1.330	1.734	2.101	2.552	2.878	3.197	3.610	3.922	
19	0.688	1.328	1.729	2.093	2.539	2.861	3.174	3.579	3.883	
20	0.687	1.325	1.725	2.086	2.528	2.845	3.153	3.552	3.850	
21	0.686	1.323	1.721	2.080	2.518	2.831	3.135	3.527	3.819	
22	0.686	1.321	1.717	2.074	2.508	2.819	3.119	3.505	3.792	
23	0.685	1.319	1.714	2.069	2.500	2.807	3.104	3.485	3.767	
24	0.685	1.318	1.711	2.064	2.492	2.797	3.091	3.467	3.745	
25	0.684	1.316	1.708	2.060	2.485	2.787	3.078	3.450	3.725	
26	0.684	1.315	1.706	2.056	2.479	2.779	3.067	3.435	3.707	
27	0.684	1.314	1.703	2.052	2.473	2.771	3.057	3.421	3.690	
28	0.683	1.313	1.701	2.048	2.467	2.763	3.047	3.408	3.674	
29	0.683	1.311	1.699	2.045	2.462	2.756	3.038	3.396	3.659	
30	0.683	1.310	1.697	2.042	2.457	2.750	3.030	3.385	3.646	4
40	0.681	1.303	1.684	2.021	2.423	2.704	2.971	3.307	3.551	3
60	0.679	1.296	1.671	2.000	2.390	2.660	2.915	3.232	3.460	2
120	0.677	1.289	1.658	1.980	2.358	2.617	2.860	3.160	3.373	1
∞	0.674	1.282	1.645	1.960	2.326	2.576	2.807	3.090	3.291	0

The tabulated function is $t_{[P]}$: if $x \sim t(v)$, Prob $(x < t_{[P]}) = P$, Prob $(x > t_{[P]}) = Q = 1 - P$, and (if $P > \frac{1}{2}$) Prob $(|x| > t_{[P]}) = 2Q$. Interpolation v-wise (for $v > 30$) should be linear in $120/v$.

Since these distributions are symmetric about the mean $t = 0$, the lower quantiles are given (for $P < \frac{1}{2}$) by:

$$t_{[P]} = -t_{[1-P]}$$

The figure shows the form of the distribution for $v = 2$; the shaded area represents the tail probability Q. For large v the distributions approximate to the normal distribution $N(0,1)$, shown by the broken line.

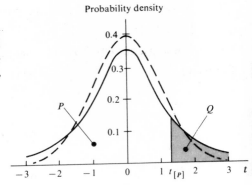

Probability density

QUANTILES $\chi^2_{[P]}$ OF CHI-SQUARE DISTRIBUTIONS $\chi^2(v)$

| P | .005 | .010 | .025 | .05 | .10 | .25 | .50 | .75 | .90 | .95 | .975 | .990 | .995 | .999 |
Q	.995	.990	.975	.95	.90	.75	.50	.25	.10	.05	.025	.010	.005	.001
$v=1$	$.0^4393$	$.0^3157$	$.0^3982$	$.0^2393$	.0158	0.102	0.455	1.323	2.706	3.841	5.024	6.635	7.879	10.83
2	.0100	.0201	.0506	0.103	0.211	0.575	1.386	2.773	4.605	5.991	7.378	9.210	10.60	13.82
3	.0717	0.115	0.216	0.352	0.584	1.213	2.366	4.108	6.251	7.815	9.348	11.34	12.84	16.27
4	0.207	0.297	0.484	0.711	1.064	1.923	3.357	5.385	7.779	9.488	11.14	13.28	14.86	18.47
5	0.412	0.554	0.831	1.145	1.610	2.675	4.351	6.626	9.236	11.07	12.83	15.09	16.75	20.52
6	0.676	0.872	1.237	1.635	2.204	3.455	5.348	7.841	10.64	12.59	14.45	16.81	18.55	22.46
7	0.989	1.239	1.690	2.167	2.833	4.255	6.346	9.037	12.02	14.07	16.01	18.48	20.28	24.32
8	1.344	1.646	2.180	2.733	3.490	5.071	7.344	10.22	13.36	15.51	17.53	20.09	21.95	26.12
9	1.735	2.088	2.700	3.325	4.168	5.899	8.343	11.39	14.68	16.92	19.02	21.67	23.59	27.88
10	2.156	2.558	3.247	3.940	4.865	6.737	9.342	12.55	15.99	18.31	20.48	23.21	25.19	29.59
11	2.603	3.053	3.816	4.575	5.578	7.584	10.34	13.70	17.28	19.68	21.92	24.73	26.76	31.26
12	3.074	3.571	4.404	5.226	6.304	8.438	11.34	14.85	18.55	21.03	23.34	26.22	28.30	32.91
13	3.565	4.107	5.009	5.892	7.042	9.299	12.34	15.98	19.81	22.36	24.74	27.69	29.82	34.53
14	4.075	4.660	5.629	6.571	7.790	10.17	13.34	17.12	21.06	23.68	26.12	29.14	31.32	36.12
15	4.601	5.229	6.262	7.261	8.547	11.04	14.34	18.25	22.31	25.00	27.49	30.58	32.80	37.70
16	5.142	5.812	6.908	7.962	9.312	11.91	15.34	19.37	23.54	26.30	28.85	32.00	34.27	39.25
17	5.697	6.408	7.564	8.672	10.09	12.79	16.34	20.49	24.77	27.59	30.19	33.41	35.72	40.79
18	6.265	7.015	8.231	9.390	10.86	13.68	17.34	21.60	25.99	28.87	31.53	34.81	37.16	42.31
19	6.844	7.633	8.907	10.12	11.65	14.56	18.34	22.72	27.20	30.14	32.85	36.19	38.58	43.82
20	7.434	8.260	9.591	10.85	12.44	15.45	19.34	23.83	28.41	31.41	34.17	37.57	40.00	45.31
21	8.034	8.897	10.28	11.59	13.24	16.34	20.34	24.93	29.62	32.67	35.48	38.93	41.40	46.80
22	8.643	9.542	10.98	12.34	14.04	17.24	21.34	26.04	30.81	33.92	36.78	40.29	42.80	48.27
23	9.260	10.20	11.69	13.09	14.85	18.14	22.34	27.14	32.01	35.17	38.08	41.64	44.18	49.73
24	9.886	10.86	12.40	13.85	15.66	19.04	23.34	28.24	33.20	36.42	39.36	42.98	45.56	51.18
25	10.52	11.52	13.12	14.61	16.47	19.94	24.34	29.34	34.38	37.65	40.65	44.31	46.93	52.62
26	11.16	12.20	13.84	15.38	17.29	20.84	25.34	30.43	35.56	38.89	41.92	45.64	48.29	54.05
27	11.81	12.88	14.57	16.15	18.11	21.75	26.34	31.53	36.74	40.11	43.19	46.96	49.64	55.48
28	12.46	13.56	15.31	16.93	18.94	22.66	27.34	32.62	37.92	41.34	44.46	48.28	50.99	56.89
29	13.12	14.26	16.05	17.71	19.77	23.57	28.34	33.71	39.09	42.56	45.72	49.59	52.34	58.30
30	13.79	14.95	16.79	18.49	20.60	24.48	29.34	34.80	40.26	43.77	46.98	50.89	53.67	59.70
40	20.71	22.16	24.43	26.51	29.05	33.66	39.34	45.62	51.81	55.76	59.34	63.69	66.77	73.40
50	27.99	29.71	32.36	34.76	37.69	42.94	49.33	56.33	63.17	67.50	71.42	76.15	79.49	86.66
60	35.53	37.48	40.48	43.19	46.46	52.29	59.33	66.98	74.40	79.08	83.30	88.38	91.95	99.61
70	43.28	45.44	48.76	51.74	55.33	61.70	69.33	77.58	85.53	90.53	95.02	100.4	104.2	112.3
80	51.17	53.54	57.15	60.39	64.28	71.14	79.33	88.13	96.58	101.9	106.6	112.3	116.3	124.8
90	59.20	61.75	65.65	69.13	73.29	80.62	89.33	98.65	107.6	113.1	118.1	124.1	128.3	137.2
100	67.33	70.06	74.22	77.93	82.36	90.13	99.33	109.1	118.5	124.3	129.6	135.8	140.2	149.4

The tabulated function is $\chi^2_{[P]}$: if $X^2 \sim \chi^2(v)$, Prob $(X^2 < \chi^2_{[P]}) = P$ and Prob $(X^2 > \chi^2_{[P]}) = Q = 1 - P$. Interpolation v-wise for $v > 30$ gives adequate values (but may lead to errors of several units in the second decimal place).

For $v > 100$ the quantiles of $\chi^2(v)$ are given approximately by

$$\chi^2_{[P]} \approx \tfrac{1}{2}\{z_{[P]} + \sqrt{(2v - 1)}\}^2$$

where $z_{[P]}$ is a quantile of $N(0,1)$.

(See p. 41.)

Probability density

[43]

QUANTILES OF SAMPLING DISTRIBUTIONS OF CORRELATION COEFFICIENTS

n	$r_{[.95]}$	$r_{[.99]}$	n	$r_{[.95]}$	$r_{[.99]}$	n	$r_{[.95]}$	$r_{[.99]}$	n	$r_{[.95]}$	$r_{[.99]}$	n	$r_{[.95]}$	$r_{[.99]}$	n	$r_{[.95]}$	$r_{[.99]}$
3	.9877	.9995	9	.582	.750	15	.441	.592	21	.369	.503	35	.283	.392	80	.185	.260
4	.9000	.9800	10	.549	.715	16	.426	.574	22	.360	.492	40	.264	.367	90	.174	.245
5	.805	.9343	11	.521	.685	17	.412	.558	23	.352	.482	45	.248	.346	100	.165	.232
6	.729	.882	12	.497	.658	18	.400	.543	24	.344	.472	50	.235	.328			
7	.669	.833	13	.476	.634	19	.389	.529	25	.337	.462	60	.214	.300			
8	.621	.789	14	.458	.612	20	.378	.516	30	.306	.423	70	.198	.278			

n	$\rho_{[.95]}$	$\rho_{[.99]}$	n	$\rho_{[.95]}$	$\rho_{[.99]}$	n	$\rho_{[.95]}$	$\rho_{[.99]}$	n	$\rho_{[.95]}$	$\rho_{[.99]}$	n	$\rho_{[.95]}$	$\rho_{[.99]}$	n	$\rho_{[.95]}$	$\rho_{[.99]}$
4	.800		9	.583	.767	14	.459	.622	19	.389	.533	24	.343	.475	29	.311	.432
5	.800	.900	10	.552	.733	15	.443	.600	20	.379	.520	25	.336	.465	30	.306	.425
6	.771	.886	11	.527	.700	16	.426	.582	21	.369	.508	26	.330	.456			
7	.679	.857	12	.497	.671	17	.412	.564	22	.360	.496	27	.324	.448			
8	.619	.810	13	.478	.643	18	.399	.548	23	.352	.485	28	.317	.440			

n	$\tau_{[.95]}$	$\tau_{[.99]}$	n	$\tau_{[.95]}$	$\tau_{[.99]}$	n	$\tau_{[.95]}$	$\tau_{[.99]}$	n	$\tau_{[.95]}$	$\tau_{[.99]}$	n	$\tau_{[.95]}$	$\tau_{[.99]}$	n	$\tau_{[.95]}$	$\tau_{[.99]}$
4	.667	1.000	11	.382	.527	18	.281	.399	25	.233	.327	32	.206	.286	39	.185	.258
5	.600	.800	12	.364	.515	19	.275	.380	26	.231	.323	33	.201	.284	40	.182	.254
6	.600	.733	13	.333	.487	20	.263	.368	27	.225	.316	34	.198	.276			
7	.524	.714	14	.341	.451	21	.257	.362	28	.222	.307	35	.193	.274			
8	.500	.643	15	.314	.448	22	.255	.351	29	.217	.305	36	.190	.270			
9	.444	.611	16	.300	.417	23	.249	.344	30	.214	.297	37	.189	.264			
10	.422	.556	17	.294	.412	24	.239	.333	31	.209	.290	38	.186	.260			

A random sample (x_i, y_i), $i = 1, 2, \ldots, n$, is taken from a bivariate population. These tables give rounded values of upper quantiles for the sample product-moment coefficient r of correlation between x and y, Spearman's correlation coefficient ρ and Kendall's correlation coefficient τ, on the hypothesis that x and y are uncorrelated in the population.

Here the quantile $\tau_{[.95]}$ for example is the largest number for which Prob $(\tau \geqslant \tau_{[.95]}) \geqslant 1 - 0.95$ or 5%, so that, if $\tau' > \tau_{[.95]}$, Prob $(\tau \geqslant \tau') < 5\%$. Similarly Prob $(\tau \geqslant \tau_{[.99]}) \geqslant 0.01$ or 1%, and, if $\tau'' > \tau_{[.99]}$, Prob $(\tau \geqslant \tau'') < 1\%$.

Since these distributions are symmetric about zero means, lower quantiles can be derived. Thus $\tau_{[.01]} = -\tau_{[.99]}$ and $\tau_{[.05]} = -\tau_{[.95]}$. Here $\tau_{[.01]}$ for example is the smallest number such that Prob $(\tau \leqslant \tau_{[.01]}) \geqslant 0.01$, and, if $\tau' < \tau_{[.01]}$, Prob $(\tau \leqslant \tau') < 1\%$.

For larger values of n, quantiles can be obtained approximately from the corresponding quantiles $z_{[P]}$ of the standardised normal distribution $N(0,1)$ (see p. 41):

$$r_{[P]} \approx \tanh \{z_{[P]}/\sqrt{(n - 3)}\} \text{ or (less accurately) } z_{[P]}/\sqrt{(n - 1)}$$

$$\rho_{[P]} \approx r_{[P]}$$

$$\tau_{[P]} \approx z_{[P]} \sqrt{\left\{\frac{2(2n + 5)}{9n(n - 1)}\right\}}$$

PROPORTIONAL PARTS FOR TENTHS

Δ	1	2	3	4	5	6	7	8	9
1	0	0	0	0	1	1	1	1	1
2	0	0	1	1	1	1	1	2	2
3	0	1	1	1	2	2	2	2	3
4	0	1	1	2	2	2	3	3	4
5	1	1	2	2	3	3	4	4	5
6	1	1	2	2	3	4	4	5	5
7	1	1	2	3	4	4	5	6	6
8	1	2	2	3	4	5	6	6	7
9	1	2	3	4	5	5	6	7	8
10	1	2	3	4	5	6	7	8	9
11	1	2	3	4	6	7	8	9	10
12	1	2	4	5	6	7	8	10	11
13	1	3	4	5	7	8	9	10	12
14	1	3	4	6	7	8	10	11	13
15	2	3	5	6	8	9	11	12	14
16	2	3	5	6	8	10	11	13	14
17	2	3	5	7	9	10	12	14	15
18	2	4	5	7	9	11	13	14	16
19	2	4	6	8	10	11	13	15	17
20	2	4	6	8	10	12	14	16	18
21	2	4	6	8	11	13	15	17	19
22	2	4	7	9	11	13	15	18	20
23	2	5	7	9	12	14	16	18	21
24	2	5	7	10	12	14	17	19	22
25	3	5	8	10	13	15	18	20	23
26	3	5	8	10	13	16	18	21	23
27	3	5	8	11	14	16	19	22	24
28	3	6	8	11	14	17	20	22	25
29	3	6	9	12	15	17	20	23	26
30	3	6	9	12	15	18	21	24	27
31	3	6	9	12	16	19	22	25	28
32	3	6	10	13	16	19	22	26	29
33	3	7	10	13	17	20	23	26	30
34	3	7	10	14	17	20	24	27	31
35	4	7	11	14	18	21	25	28	32
36	4	7	11	14	18	22	25	29	32
37	4	7	11	15	19	22	26	30	33
38	4	8	11	15	19	23	27	30	34
39	4	8	12	16	20	23	27	31	35
40	4	8	12	16	20	24	28	32	36
41	4	8	12	16	21	25	29	33	37
42	4	8	13	17	21	25	29	34	38
43	4	9	13	17	22	26	30	34	39
44	4	9	13	18	22	26	31	35	40
45	5	9	14	18	23	27	32	36	41
46	5	9	14	18	23	28	32	37	41
47	5	9	14	19	24	28	33	38	42
48	5	10	14	19	24	29	34	38	43
49	5	10	15	20	25	29	34	39	44
50	5	10	15	20	25	30	35	40	45

Δ	1	2	3	4	5	6	7	8	9
51	5	10	15	20	26	31	36	41	46
52	5	10	16	21	26	31	36	42	47
53	5	11	16	21	27	32	37	42	48
54	5	11	16	22	27	32	38	43	49
55	6	11	17	22	28	33	39	44	50
56	6	11	17	22	28	34	39	45	50
57	6	11	17	23	29	34	40	46	51
58	6	12	17	23	29	35	41	46	52
59	6	12	18	24	30	35	41	47	53
60	6	12	18	24	30	36	42	48	54
61	6	12	18	24	31	37	43	49	55
62	6	12	19	25	31	37	43	50	56
63	6	13	19	25	32	38	44	50	57
64	6	13	19	26	32	38	45	51	58
65	7	13	20	26	33	39	46	52	59
66	7	13	20	26	33	40	46	53	59
67	7	13	20	27	34	40	47	54	60
68	7	14	20	27	34	41	48	54	61
69	7	14	21	28	35	41	48	55	62
70	7	14	21	28	35	42	49	56	63
71	7	14	21	28	36	43	50	57	64
72	7	14	22	29	36	43	50	58	65
73	7	15	22	29	37	44	51	58	66
74	7	15	22	30	37	44	52	59	67
75	8	15	23	30	38	45	53	60	68
76	8	15	23	30	38	46	53	61	68
77	8	15	23	31	39	46	54	62	69
78	8	16	23	31	39	47	55	62	70
79	8	16	24	32	40	47	55	63	71
80	8	16	24	32	40	48	56	64	72
81	8	16	24	32	41	49	57	65	73
82	8	16	25	33	41	49	57	66	74
83	8	17	25	33	42	50	58	66	75
84	8	17	25	34	42	50	59	67	76
85	9	17	26	34	43	51	60	68	77
86	9	17	26	34	43	52	60	69	77
87	9	17	26	35	44	52	61	70	78
88	9	18	26	35	44	53	62	70	79
89	9	18	27	36	45	53	62	71	80
90	9	18	27	36	45	54	63	72	81
91	9	18	27	36	46	55	64	73	82
92	9	18	28	37	46	55	64	74	83
93	9	19	28	37	47	56	65	74	84
94	9	19	28	38	47	56	66	75	85
95	10	19	29	38	48	57	67	76	86
96	10	19	29	38	48	58	67	77	86
97	10	19	29	39	49	58	68	78	87
98	10	20	29	39	49	59	69	78	88
99	10	20	30	40	50	59	69	79	89
100	10	20	30	40	50	60	70	80	90

Δ	1	2	3	4	5	6	7	8	9
101	10	20	30	40	51	61	71	81	91
102	10	20	31	41	51	61	71	82	92
103	10	21	31	41	52	62	72	82	93
104	10	21	31	42	52	62	73	83	94
105	11	21	32	42	53	63	74	84	95
106	11	21	32	42	53	64	74	85	95
107	11	21	32	43	54	64	75	86	96
108	11	22	32	43	54	65	76	86	97
109	11	22	33	44	55	65	76	87	98
110	11	22	33	44	55	66	77	88	99
111	11	22	33	44	56	67	78	89	100
112	11	22	34	45	56	67	78	90	101
113	11	23	34	45	57	68	79	90	102
114	11	23	34	46	57	68	80	91	103
115	12	23	35	46	58	69	81	92	104
116	12	23	35	46	58	70	81	93	104
117	12	23	35	47	59	70	82	94	105
118	12	24	35	47	59	71	83	94	106
119	12	24	36	48	60	71	83	95	107
120	12	24	36	48	60	72	84	96	108
121	12	24	36	48	61	73	85	97	109
122	12	24	37	49	61	73	85	98	110
123	12	25	37	49	62	74	86	98	111
124	12	25	37	50	62	74	87	99	112
125	13	25	38	50	63	75	88	100	113
126	13	25	38	50	63	76	88	101	113
127	13	25	38	51	64	76	89	102	114
128	13	26	38	51	64	77	90	102	115
129	13	26	39	52	65	77	90	103	116
130	13	26	39	52	65	78	91	104	117
131	13	26	39	52	66	79	92	105	118
132	13	26	40	53	66	79	92	106	119
133	13	27	40	53	67	80	93	106	120
134	13	27	40	54	67	80	94	107	121
135	14	27	41	54	68	81	95	108	122
136	14	27	41	54	68	82	95	109	122
137	14	27	41	55	69	82	96	110	123
138	14	28	41	55	69	83	97	110	124
139	14	28	42	56	70	83	97	111	125
140	14	28	42	56	70	84	98	112	126
141	14	28	42	56	71	85	99	113	127
142	14	28	43	57	71	85	99	114	128
143	14	29	43	57	72	86	100	114	129
144	14	29	43	58	72	86	101	115	130
145	15	29	44	58	73	87	102	116	131
146	15	29	44	58	73	88	102	117	131
147	15	29	44	59	74	88	103	118	132
148	15	30	44	59	74	89	104	118	133
149	15	30	45	60	75	89	104	119	134
150	15	30	45	60	75	90	105	120	135

If successive tabular entries y_1 and $y_2 = y_1 + \Delta$ correspond to values x_1 and $x_2 = x_1 + h$, respectively, of the independent variable, the value y corresponding to the value $x = x_1 + ph$, where $0 < p < 1$, is approximately $y_1 + p\Delta$. This table gives the values of $p\Delta$ for $p = 0.1, 0.2, \ldots, 0.9$ and $\Delta = 1, 2, \ldots, 150$.

INTERNATIONAL SYSTEM OF UNITS (SI)

Physical quantity	Unit	Symbol	Equivalent form
Length (l, x)	metre	m	⎫
Mass (M, m)	kilogram	kg	
Time (t)	second	s	Base
Electric current (I)	ampere	A	units
Thermodynamic temperature (T)	kelvin	K	
Luminous intensity (I)	candela	cd	
Amount of substance (n, v)	mole	mol	⎭
Frequency, cycles per sec. (f, v)	hertz	Hz	s^{-1}
Force (F)	newton	N	$kg\ m\ s^{-2}$
Pressure (p, P)	pascal	Pa	$N\ m^{-2}$
Work, energy (W, E, U), quantity of heat (Q)	joule	J	$N\ m$
Power (P)	watt	W	$J\ s^{-1}$
Electric charge (Q)	coulomb	C	$A\ s$
Electric potential, p.d., e.m.f. (φ, V)	volt	V	$J\ C^{-1}, W\ A^{-1}$
Capacitance (C)	farad	F	$C\ V^{-1}$
Electric resistance (R)	ohm	Ω	$V\ A^{-1}$
Electric conductance (G)	siemens	S	$Ω^{-1}$
Magnetic flux (Φ)	weber	Wb	$V\ s$
Magnetic flux density (B)	tesla	T	$Wb\ m^{-2}$
Inductance (L)	henry	H	$Wb\ A^{-1}$

Multiples and submultiples: Prefixes are used to indicate multiples (and submultiples) of units (e.g. microfarad, μF). The following prefixes are in general use:

Factor	10^{12}	10^{9}	10^{6}	10^{3}	10^{-3}	10^{-6}	10^{-9}	10^{-12}
Prefix	tera	giga	mega	kilo	milli	micro	nano	pico
Symbol	T	G	M	k	m	μ	n	p

The prefixes for 10^{-1} (deci, d), 10^{-2} (centi, c) and some others are used less widely.

Compound units can be formed from multiples of named units (e.g. km s^{-2}), but prefixes are not used to denote multiples of compound units.

OTHER UNITS

Unit	SI equivalent	Unit	SI equivalent
Length		*Mass and density*	
ångström (Å)	0.1 nm	gram (g)	10^{-3} kg
inch (in)	25.4 mm	tonne (t)	10^{3} kg
foot (ft)	0.3048 m	ounce (oz)	28.35 g
yard	0.9144 m	pound (lb)	0.4536 kg
mile	1.6093 km	ton	1.016 t
nautical mile (Int.)	1.852 km	lb ft^{-3}	16.02 kg m^{-3}
Area		*Force*	
hectare (ha)	10^{4} m^{2}	poundal (pdl)	0.1383 N
square foot	9.290×10^{-2} m^{2}	lbf	4.448 N
acre	0.4047 ha	tonf	9.964 kN
Volume		*Energy and power*	
litre (l)	1 dm^{3} or 10^{-3} m^{3}	ft pdl	0.04214 J
millilitre (ml)	1 cm^{3} or 10^{-6} m^{3}	ft lbf	1.356 J
cubic foot	2.832×10^{-2} m^{3}	calorie 15 °C (cal$_{15}$)	4.1855 J
pint	0.568 l	calorie I.T. (cal$_{IT}$)	4.1868 J
gallon (UK)	4.546 l	Btu	1.055 kJ
gallon (US)	3.785 l	horsepower (hp)	745.7 W
Speed		*Pressure and stress*	
km/hour	0.2778 m s^{-1}	bar	10^{5} Pa
mile/hour (m.p.h.)	0.4470 m s^{-1}	atmosphere (atm)	101.33 kPa
foot/second	0.3048 m s^{-1}	torr (mmHg)	133.3 Pa
knot (UK)	0.5148 m s^{-1}	lbf in^{-2} (p.s.i.)	6.895 kPa
rev/min (r.p.m.)	0.1047 rad s^{-1}	tonf ft^{-2}	107.3 kPa

PHYSICAL CONSTANTS

Temperature
Zero of the Celsius scale (0°C) 273.15 K

Earth, Moon and Sun
Mass of Earth 5.97×10^{24} kg, Moon 7.33×10^{22} kg, Sun 1.99×10^{30} kg
Mean radius of Earth 6.37×10^6 m, Moon 1.74×10^6 m, Sun 6.96×10^8 m
Distance of Earth to Moon 3.84×10^8 m, to Sun 1.50×10^{11} m
Gravitational constant $G = 6.673 \times 10^{-11}$ N m² kg⁻²
Acceleration of free fall on surface of Moon $g = 1.62$ m s⁻²; on the Earth, at height z m in
  latitude φ, $g = (9.7805 + 0.0517 \sin^2 \varphi - 3 \times 10^{-6} z)$ m s⁻²

Molar constants
Molar volume (at s.t.p.) $V_m = 2.241 \times 10^{-2}$ m³ mol⁻¹
Avogadro constant N_A or $L = 6.022 \times 10^{23}$ mol⁻¹
Boltzmann constant $k = 1.381 \times 10^{-23}$ J K⁻¹
Gas constant $R = L k = 8.314$ J K⁻¹ mol⁻¹
Faraday constant $F = L e = 9.649 \times 10^4$ C mol⁻¹

Electrical, optical and atomic constants
Permittivity of empty space $\varepsilon_0 = 10^7/4\pi c^2$ F m⁻¹ $= 8.854 \times 10^{-12}$ F m⁻¹
Permeability of empty space $\mu_0 = 4\pi \times 10^{-7}$ H m⁻¹ $= 1.2566 \times 10^{-6}$ H m⁻¹
Impedance of empty space $Z_0 = (\mu_0/\varepsilon_0)^{1/2} = 376.7$ Ω
Speed of light $c = (\varepsilon_0 \mu_0)^{-1/2} = 2.998 \times 10^8$ m s⁻¹; light-year $= 9.46 \times 10^{15}$ m
Stefan–Boltzmann constant $\sigma = 5.670 \times 10^{-8}$ W m⁻² K⁻⁴
Wien's radiation law: $\lambda_{max} T = 2.898 \times 10^{-3}$ m K; $\nu_{max}/T = 5.879 \times 10^{10}$ s⁻¹ K⁻¹
Rydberg constant $R_\infty = 1.0974 \times 10^7$ m⁻¹
Wavelengths of Fraunhofer lines: Na D (yellow) 589.6 nm, 589.0 nm;
  H C (red) 656.3 nm; H F (blue-green) 486.1 nm
Mass of proton 1.6726×10^{-27} kg, neutron 1.6749×10^{-27} kg, electron 9.110×10^{-31} kg
Charge of proton or electron $\pm e = \pm 1.602 \times 10^{-19}$ C
Specific charge of electron $-e/m = -1.759 \times 10^{11}$ C kg⁻¹
Planck constant $h = 6.626 \times 10^{-34}$ J s, $\hbar = h/2\pi = 1.0546 \times 10^{-34}$ J s

Air and water
Density $\rho/$(kg m⁻³): dry air (s.t.p.) 1.293, (20 °C, 1 atm) 1.205;
  water (0 °C) 0.99984×10^3, (20 °C) 0.99820×10^3; ice (0 °C) 0.917×10^3
Speed of sound $c/$(m s⁻¹): air (α °C) $331.5 + 0.61\alpha$; water (0 °C) 1403, (20 °C) 1483
Viscosity $\eta/$(Pa s): air (0 °C) 1.71×10^{-5}, (20 °C) 1.81×10^{-5};
  water (0 °C) 1.79×10^{-3}, (20 °C) 1.00×10^{-3}, (100 °C) 0.28×10^{-3}
Surface tension $\gamma/$(N m⁻¹): water/air (20 °C) 7.3×10^{-2}, (100 °C) 5.9×10^{-2}
Specific heat capacity $c/$(kJ kg⁻¹ K⁻¹): water (20 °C) 4.182; ice (0 °C) 2.09;
  air $c_p/$(kJ kg⁻¹ K⁻¹) $= 1.008$, $c_p/c_V = 1.40$
Specific latent heat $l/$(kJ kg⁻¹): ice/water 333.5; water/vapour (100 °C) 2256
Thermal conductivity $\lambda/$(W m⁻¹ K⁻¹): air (0 °C) 2.4×10^{-2}; water (20 °C) 0.60; ice 2.2
Refractive index: air (s.t.p.) for Na D 1.000292; ice for Na D 1.31;
  water (20 °C) for H C 1.331, Na D 1.333, H F 1.337

Other materials
The properties of these materials vary widely, and their values may differ considerably from
the typical values given, which correspond to a temperature of about 20 °C.

Density $\rho/$(10³ kg m⁻³): aluminium 2.7, cast iron 7.6, copper 8.9, glass 2.6, lead 11.3,
  mercury 13.5, mild steel 7.8, oak 0.8, paraffin oil 0.8, PVC 1.3, softwood 0.5
Young modulus $E/$(10¹⁰ Pa): aluminium 7.0, copper 12, mild steel 22, oak 1.3
Bulk modulus $K/$(10¹⁰ Pa): aluminium 7.5, copper 13.5, mild steel 16.0
Shear modulus $G/$(10¹⁰ Pa): aluminium 2.5, copper 4.4, mild steel 8.0
Thermal conductivity $\lambda/$(W m⁻¹ K⁻¹): aluminium 2.4×10^2, brick 0.5, concrete 1.05,
  copper 3.8×10^2, cork 0.05, glass wool 0.04, soda glass 0.71, pyrex 1.1, steel 46
Linear expansivity $\alpha/$(10⁻⁶ K⁻¹): brass 19, brick 9.5, concrete 12, copper 16.7,
  glass (soft) 8.5, invar 1, mild steel 12, nylon 100, pyrex glass 3
Specific heat capacity $c/$(kJ kg⁻¹ K⁻¹): aluminium 0.91, brass 0.39, copper 0.385,
  glass (soft) 0.67, nylon 2.3, PVC 1.1, pyrex 0.78, paraffin oil 2.2, steel 0.45, wood 1.7
Refractive index: diamond 2.42, fused quartz 1.46, glass 1.5 to 1.9, perspex 1.50
Electric resistivity of conductors $\rho/$(10⁻⁸ Ω m): aluminium 2.6, brass 8, constantan 49,
  copper 1.7, lead 20, mercury 96, manganin 44, mild steel 15
Electric resistivity of insulators $\rho/$(Ω m): glass plate 2×10^{11}, nylon 10^{11}, paraffin wax
  3×10^{16}, porcelain 3×10^{12}, fused quartz $> 10^{16}$, sealing wax $\sim 10^{14}$, sulphur $\sim 10^{15}$.
The resistance of most insulators decreases extremely rapidly with temperature.

Published by the Press Syndicate of the University of Cambridge
The Pitt Building, Trumpington Street, Cambridge CB2 1RP
32 East 57th Street, New York, NY 10022, USA
296 Beaconsfield Parade, Middle Park, Melbourne 3206, Australia

First published 1965
Reprinted 1967, 1974, 1975, 1978
Second edition 1979
Reprinted 1980, 1981

Printed in Great Britain by
Richard Clay (The Chaucer Press), Ltd
Bungay, Suffolk

ISBN 0 521 22255 9
(ISBN 0 521 05728 0 first edition)